RONALD REAGAN

Ronald REAGAN

by Rebecca Larsen

An Impact Biography

FRANKLIN WATTS
New York ■ Chicago ■ London ■ Toronto ■ Sydney

Photographs copyright ©: The Ronald Reagan Library: pp. 11, 47 top, 61, 120, 176 (Jack Kightlinger); The Bettmann Archive: p. 15; AP/Wide World Photos: pp. 23, 35, 47 bottom, 55, 58, 65, 76, 81, 94, 98, 104, 126, 150; Archive Photos, NYC: pp. 33, 147; UPI/Bettmann Newsphotos: pp. 38, 42, 46, 73, 91, 108, 117, 133, 136, 142; Gamma-Liaison/Markel: p. 169; Randy Matusow: p. 174.

Library of Congress Cataloging-in-Publication Data

Larsen, Rebecca.
Ronald Reagan / by Rebecca Larsen.
p.   cm.—(An Impact biography)
Includes bibliographical references and index.
ISBN 0-531-11191-1 (lib. bdg.)
1. Reagan, Ronald—Juvenile literature. 2. Presidents—United States—Biography—Juvenile literature. [1. Reagan, Ronald. 2. Presidents.] I. Title.
E877.137 1994
973.927′092—dc20
[B]   94-19543 CIP AC

CONTENTS

CHAPTER ONE
DUTCH
9

CHAPTER TWO
PLAY-BY-PLAY
20

CHAPTER THREE
TROUBLE AT HOME AND ABROAD
29

CHAPTER FOUR
SCREEN IDLE
40

CHAPTER FIVE
BEARING RIGHT
49

CHAPTER SIX
MR. GOVERNOR
59

CHAPTER SEVEN
WHO, ME?
70

CHAPTER EIGHT
WOUNDED, NOT SLAIN
78

CHAPTER NINE
"THERE YOU GO AGAIN"   85

CHAPTER TEN
"TIME TO REAWAKEN
THIS INDUSTRIAL GIANT"   97

CHAPTER ELEVEN
FOREIGN AFFAIRS   114

CHAPTER TWELVE
MORNING AGAIN
IN AMERICA   122

CHAPTER THIRTEEN
COVERT OPERATIONS   128

CHAPTER FOURTEEN
NEGOTIATING WITH
TERRORISTS   138

CHAPTER FIFTEEN
ON HIS WATCH   149

CHAPTER SIXTEEN
BREAKING DOWN WALLS   160

EPILOGUE   172

SOURCE NOTES   177

BIBLIOGRAPHY   183

INDEX   185

RONALD REAGAN

CHAPTER ONE
DUTCH

One chilly winter night in Dixon, Illinois, eleven-year-old Ronald Reagan came home to a darkened house; everyone else was out for the evening. As the boy, nicknamed Dutch by his family and friends, climbed the steps to the door he almost stumbled over someone lying on the porch. It was his father, Jack, flat on his back and snoring.

Ronald knew what the problem was; his mother, Nelle, had explained that his father had a sickness, an addiction to alcohol, something he couldn't control. At times he had heard his parents arguing over Jack's drinking, but now for the first time, he was facing his father's problem.

At first he was terrified and wanted to run away, but he couldn't leave his father lying there drunk. He grabbed Jack by his overcoat, pulled him inside the house, and put him into a bed.

It was a harsh moment of reality for a boy who always had a happy view of the future, who expected the very best to come to him in life. Somehow, though, he managed to put the incident behind him and to keep his affection for his father alive. He loved his father's feistiness and Irish jokes and stories; he admired his political beliefs. But like many children of alcoholic parents, he often had the threat of his father's drinking bouts on his mind.

Ronald Wilson Reagan had been born on February 6, 1911, in tiny Tampico, Illinois (population 820), in an upstairs apartment on the town's main street. He weighed ten pounds, and his father had joked: "He looks like a fat little Dutchman."[1] That's how the nickname Dutch had come to be. The Reagans had another son, Neil, who was two years older; Ronald would be his parents' last child.

Although the Reagans were not homeless or starving, life was always a struggle for them. Both John Edward Reagan, known as Jack, and his wife, Nelle Wilson Reagan, had had only a few years of grade school education. Jack was a Catholic who attended Mass now and then; Nelle was a devoted member of the Disciples of Christ, or Christian, church. Both had lost their parents when they were young; both had to work hard to keep their families going.

Jack was a Democrat and believed strongly in the equality of all men. For example, he had refused to let his boys see *The Birth of a Nation* at a local theater because he believed the film glorified the Ku Klux Klan and its violence toward blacks. He also clung to the American dream—the belief that those who work hard will prosper. But success eluded Jack, even though his goal—to own his own shoe store—was a modest one.

For years the family moved from town to town in Illinois as Jack tried to find better jobs in retail sales. His drinking habit hindered his work at times. From Tampico they went to Chicago and then on to Galesburg. Then it was on to Monmouth and back to Tampico and finally to Dixon, where Ronald spent most of his boyhood. Dixon lay on the Rock River in a rich farm area, but most of its residents were not much better off than the Reagans. To young Dutch, the town was an amazing sight.

John Edward Reagan and his wife, Nelle, pose with their children, Ronald (left) and Neil, in a portrait taken around 1913.

"Dixon was more than ten times larger than Tampico. We arrived there in 1920 when I was nine years old, and to me it was heaven," Reagan later said.[2]

As the boys grew older, Dutch naturally took second place to his older brother who was larger, stronger, and more athletic. Neil was livelier and more mischievous and tended to spend more time with their father. Dutch was a quiet dreamer, more interested in what his mother did and in her church. Dutch also loved to study a collection of birds' eggs and butterflies that the Reagans had found in one of the houses they rented while trekking from city to city.

One day before he was old enough for school, Dutch was lying on the floor and studying a newspaper when his father walked into the room. When his father asked him what he was doing, he replied, "Reading the paper."

Jack asked him to read a few sentences, and Dutch did so. "The next thing I knew, he was flying out the front door and from the porch inviting all our neighbors to come over and hear his five-year-old son read."[3] Apparently Dutch had learned how to decode words and letters while listening to his mother read bedtime stories.

After that, Dutch proved to be a polite and good student in elementary school. He had almost a photographic memory for dates and names; he learned to add, subtract, and multiply quickly. His teachers liked him, and he even skipped a grade in elementary school. His success was all the more amazing because he was very nearsighted, and his parents didn't learn that he needed glasses until he was a teenager.

Dutch kept to himself a lot and was wild about reading adventure stories like the Tarzan books. But he loved rough physical play, too. He was a good swimmer, and although skinny for his age, he threw himself wildly into football games with his brother and their friends.

Nelle Reagan raised both boys in her church. The three of them went to Sunday school, two church services on Sunday, and prayer meetings on Wednesdays. Dutch took his mother's faith seriously and "invited" Christ into his life when he was baptized into the church in 1922.[4] As a teenager he taught Sunday school and led some prayer meetings. In his talks he often used examples of athletes to illustrate stories about Christian living. Already he had a good speaking voice and a way of making Bible lessons come alive. Many people thought he had inherited this gift from his mother who was known for her dramatic readings. He might make a good minister someday, they thought.

Nelle Reagan persuaded her sons to give speeches at the drama evenings where she also performed. The first time he spoke in public Dutch was nervous, but his anxiety faded when he heard the audience laugh and clap. "For a kid suffering childhood pangs of insecurity, the applause was music," he said.[5]

Soon Dutch entered North Dixon High School. Although he had grown taller and more muscular, he weighed only 108 pounds and was five feet three inches tall. That did not stop him from trying out for the football team. Nor was he deterred when he sat on the bench for most of the games during the first two years. His persistence eventually won him a spot as a first-string guard on the team.

The summer after his sophomore year, Dutch became a lifeguard in the Rock River swimming area in Lowell Park, a forest preserve in the middle of Dixon. He started at fifteen dollars a week and worked his way up to twenty. On especially hot days, it was a twelve-hour job. It was a difficult area to swim in, and often Dutch jumped in to "save" swimmers, although sometimes the swimmers objected that they really didn't need his help. He carved marks on a log next to the river to show how many swimmers he had "saved." After several summers on the job, he had seventy-six notches.

That first summer as a lifeguard he met his first girlfriend, Margaret Cleaver, the daughter of the minister at his church. The two often paddled a canoe on the river. Dutch took along a portable Victrola and played his favorite record, "Ramona," over and over again.

In addition to joining the high school football team, Dutch acted regularly in school plays and became president of the dramatics club. "He possessed a sense of presence on the stage, a sense of reality. . . . He fit into almost any kind of role you put him into," said the high school English teacher, B. J. Frazer, who supervised the club.[6]

Frazer taught him how to get inside a character's skin, Reagan said later. Soon Dutch was reading new scripts and trying to understand what his character's motivations were.

In high school Dutch was a good student but not an outstanding one. He preferred his out-of-class activities. He was elected president of the senior class and became art editor of the school yearbook. He also wrote essays and poems for school publications.

Although football was his favorite sport, Reagan was an excellent swimmer. During his school years, he worked for seven summers as a lifeguard at Lowell Park, in Dixon, Illinois.

14

As high school drew to a close, Dutch worried over his future. He had always talked about college, and his mother had encouraged both boys to think about more schooling. But where would the money come from? Jack Reagan's job had not gone well in Dixon, and the family had moved to a smaller house to cut their rent. The boys had to sleep on an enclosed but unheated porch year-round.

When Neil graduated from high school, he went straight to work at a local cement company where he made $125 a month and helped meet the family's expenses.

By the end of the summer after graduation in 1928, Dutch had saved $400, not even enough to get through the first year of school. But in the fall, when Margaret Cleaver set off for Eureka College, the Disciples of Christ school about a hundred miles from Dixon, Dutch climbed in the car, too. He was determined to arrange a way to go to the school. When he saw the campus, he fell in love with it. The school's graceful Colonial-style brick buildings were covered with ivy. Lush rolling lawns and beautiful trees covered the campus, which was surrounded by farms.

Tuition at Eureka, a tiny school with only 220 students, was $180, and Dutch got an athletic scholarship for half that. He was accepted in the Tau Kappa Epsilon fraternity and moved into the fraternity house, where he washed dishes and waited on tables in return for meals. His room in the house cost $270. Paying his bills was a financial struggle for him, but most students on campus came from low-income families, so almost all of them had to work to pay their bills.

Dutch's freshman classes included French, history, rhetoric, English literature, and math; he ended up majoring in economics. His first year he earned only passing grades although he could have done much better. From the start, he was most interested in the sports and activities on campus. At a small school, a student could try everything. Even so, Dutch found it tough going on the football team. He was tall but thin. With his glasses off, he could hardly see the football or the players in front of him. According to the coach, Dutch was a fifth-stringer and never played in any close games in his first year on the squad. He worked hard in practices, but football was an important sport at Eureka, and the coach could not gamble on giving Dutch a chance to play. He did much better in swimming where his lifeguarding experience helped make him the star of the team.

Although he was only a freshman, Dutch got a taste of campus politics before the first semester ended. Just before Thanksgiving, Bert Wilson, the college president, proposed to trustees that they cut back faculty and classes because donations to the school had dropped off. The cuts were supposed to take place while students were home for the holiday.

As the news spread, the campus went into an uproar. Teachers were angry about losing their jobs; students were afraid they could not graduate in four years if classes were cut. Many thought Wilson should have asked for their advice before moving so drastically. Students were also getting angry about the strict rules at the religious school—including a ban on dancing and smoking on campus.

Irate students and teachers flocked to a late evening rally the night before Thanksgiving vacation. Although just a freshman, Dutch spoke for a committee of students who proposed going on strike to force the administration to listen to them. Giving the speech and urging the students to join the boycott was a heady moment for Dutch. The applause and yells thundered through the college chapel. "For the first time in my life, I felt my words reach out and grab an audience, and it was exhilarating," he said.[7]

The strike took place after vacation. Only six students attended classes, and reporters from around the state flocked to Eureka to interview strikers and trustees. Eventually the president quit, and students went back to classes. They had won the battle: no classes were cut and some rules were changed; dances could even be held on campus.

Although he loved Eureka, when Dutch went home for the summer to work as a lifeguard again, he feared he wouldn't have enough money to return to school in the fall. His savings were gone, and his family was still desperate for money. At summer's end he was ready to take a job with a land surveyor who promised to get him a University of Wisconsin scholarship if he would work for a year. But at the last minute Margaret Cleaver talked him into returning to school to arrange new scholarships. Her suggestion worked; the football coach got him a new grant for half his tuition, and the college deferred the rest of his tuition until after graduation. He got a job washing dishes in a girls' dormitory. He also arranged a football scholarship for Neil, who was soon washing dishes in the Tau Kappa Epsilon house, as Dutch had once done.

During the next three years at Eureka, Dutch scrambled to play first string on the football team. He competed in track and swimming, served in the student senate, and was student body president— all that plus working on the yearbook and serving as a basketball cheerleader. His grades were less important to him, although he earned better than a C average. Perhaps because of his experiences with his father, Dutch experimented only a little with alcohol at college. Throughout his life, he seldom drank more than a single glass of wine or liquor in an evening.

One of his greatest loves was acting in plays with the drama society. In his junior year he and the group competed in a one-act play contest at Northwestern University. Eureka placed second, and Dutch received an individual acting award. By senior year he was secretly daydreaming about becoming a movie actor.

But Hollywood and the movies seemed a long way off in those days. When Dutch was ready to graduate, the nation had been hard hit by the Great Depression. The Reagan family especially felt the pinch. The store that Jack Reagan managed had shut down, and he became a traveling salesman, paid on commission only. Nelle Reagan worked as a seamstress in a dress shop. One Christmas Eve, in fact, a special delivery letter came for Jack. He was expecting a Christmas bonus from his new company; instead he got a notice that he had been laid off. The Reagan family finances got so bad that Nelle and Jack lived for a while in one room of an apartment rented to someone else and cooked on a hot plate.

When Dutch graduated in the spring of 1932, only forty-five students were left in his class. Many had dropped out because of financial problems, and some graduates still owed the school money. As a class officer, Dutch spoke at commencement on a beautiful spring day on campus. The graduates were excited and full of high hopes, but the nation was in deep trouble, and no one knew what troubles or success lay ahead.

CHAPTER TWO
PLAY-BY-PLAY

When Dutch Reagan left college in 1932, his forty-nine-year-old father was out of work and looking for a job. His mother was eking out a salary in a dress shop, and the boys had come home to Dixon to take summer jobs. With their combined salaries, they could only afford a two-bedroom apartment, and Jack had hung on to a battered Oldsmobile to drive to job interviews. Dutch was a lifeguard again, but he had bigger ideas.

He was afraid to tell anyone his most fantastic dream—to go to Hollywood and become an actor. Instead he picked a goal a little closer to home—to become a radio sports announcer. After all, the infant radio industry was growing quickly, and new jobs were being created all the time. Chicago, just a few hundred miles from Dixon, was a center of radio broadcasting. An older friend of Dutch suggested he visit all of the radio stations to ask for a job. Be ready to take any work to break into broadcasting, he told the young man.

At summer's end, with his job as a lifeguard coming to a close, Dutch set off to give radio a try. He told his mother that he was going to hitchhike to Chicago and knock on doors. He was hesitant to tell his father about the trip.

He quickly caught a ride to Chicago, but once he got there his luck ran out. He went from one radio station to another without landing an interview. Finally an official at the NBC station told him it was a poor idea to hunt for a job in a big city, because he lacked experience. He needed to try small stations in small towns first.

Tired and discouraged, Dutch hitchhiked back to Dixon after a few days with nothing to show for his efforts. Things did not get better back home, either. Montgomery Ward was opening a brand-new department store in town and wanted an athletic young man to manage its sporting goods department. Dutch rushed down to the store and ended up as one of two finalists for the job. But the store hired the other young man, a former superstar on Reagan's high school basketball team. Dutch was crushed and confessed to his father about his disappointing trip to Chicago. Jack urged him to try other radio stations and lent him his car for the job hunt.

Dutch's first stop was about seventy miles from his home, at WOC in Davenport, Iowa, a city of about 70,000 on the Mississippi River. The station there was owned by the Palmer School of Chiropractic and the call letters stood for "World of Chiropractic." In fact, the station was on the top floor of the school. There Dutch met Peter MacArthur, the station manager and a former vaudeville performer who had originally come to the school to get medical help for arthritis. MacArthur gruffly told Reagan he was too late; the station had advertised for a month for an announcer and had just hired one. Disappointed once again, Reagan headed for the elevator while grumbling, "How the hell can you get to be a sports announcer if you can't even get a job at a radio station?"[1]

Using two canes, MacArthur shuffled after

Dutch to ask the young man if he had been talking about sports announcing. After Dutch explained his sports background and his goal of announcing games, MacArthur asked in his Scottish burr: "Could ye tell me about a football game and make me see it as if I was home listening to the radio?"[2]

Dutch said he could; so then and there MacArthur took him into a studio and put him in front of a microphone. Dutch then gave a play-by-play version of one of his last football games at Eureka against Western State University—complete with details on weather and the stadium.

When he had finished, MacArthur threw open the studio door and yelled, "Ye did great." Dutch was hired to broadcast the Iowa-Minnesota homecoming game the next Saturday.

It wasn't exactly a full-time job, just five dollars plus bus fare for the game, but he had a chance to prove himself. During the week, Reagan studied the teams and players and then on Saturday went to Iowa City with another announcer. He threw himself into the assignment, and when it was over, MacArthur told him he could broadcast Iowa's remaining games for ten dollars each. Finally Dutch could call himself a sports announcer.

When the season ended, Dutch was offered a staff announcer's job paying $100 a month. He rented a room for $8.00 a week and got his meals at the chiropractic school for $3.65 a week. He also sent

During the early 1930s, Reagan worked as a sports announcer for WHO radio in Des Moines, Iowa, covering the Chicago Cubs baseball team. He became widely known for the amusing way he filled in details for his radio audience.

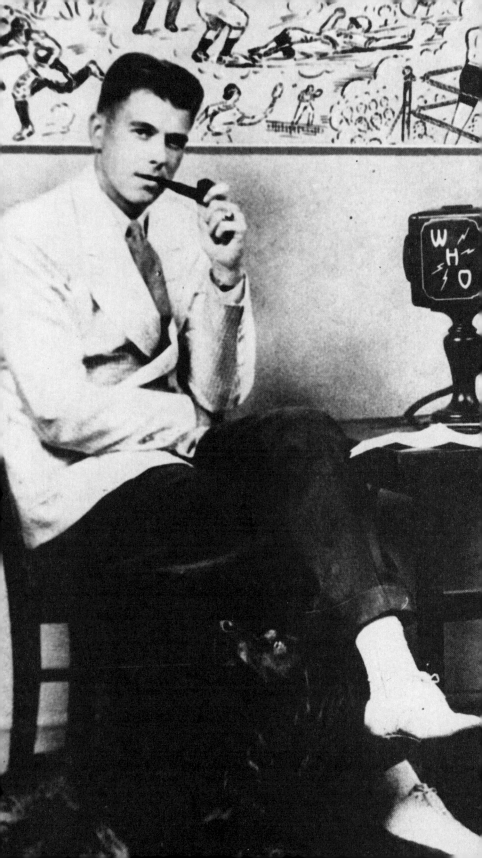

money to his parents and to his brother, who was still a Eureka student. The situation at home improved after Franklin Delano Roosevelt was elected president. Jack had been an enthusiastic Democratic Party worker for FDR, and the entire family, including Dutch, had voted for Roosevelt. After the new president took office, Jack was given a job with the county supervisor of poor, helping distribute food to the unemployed. The affection that Dutch, too, had developed for Roosevelt would last throughout his life.

In his new job as a WOC announcer, Dutch got off to a wobbly start. His job was to spin records and read commercials for a local funeral home and other businesses, and he bumbled and stumbled along. His delivery was stilted, and he even left out a commercial for the mortuary when he thought it did not sound right. It seemed hard to believe, but Dutch Reagan, the same young man who had roused college audiences with his speeches, was almost tongue-tied on the air. After three weeks, the station decided to get rid of him. But Dutch's replacement did not work out, either, and so Dutch was asked to stay after all. The second time around, people at the station helped him improve his delivery. His natural gift for talking off the cuff—spinning entertaining stories and making people chuckle—took hold.

Soon WOC merged with a larger station, WHO in Des Moines, Iowa. The Palmer Company, which owned both stations, made Reagan a sports announcer with WHO. He had taken a big step up in the world: Des Moines was twice as big as Davenport and the station was one of the largest NBC stations in the nation. WHO broadcast throughout the Midwest, carrying such popular comedy shows as *Fibber McGee and Molly* and *The Great Gildersleeve.*

His salary climbed to $75 a week, and he was doing work he loved—attending football games, track meets, swimming events, and auto races and announcing them for the radio. He even got his brother an announcing job in radio, too. He had a romantic disappointment, though. His high school and college sweetheart, Margaret, had gone to Europe for a year of study. Before leaving, she sent him back his fraternity pin and engagement ring. In spite of that, Reagan still thought things would work out and that they would marry someday.

Then there was a shock: Margaret wrote to Reagan to say she had met a foreign service officer whom she planned to marry. "Margaret's decision shattered me," Reagan said, "not so much, I think, because she no longer loved me, but because I no longer had anyone to love."[3]

Gradually he adjusted, however. He had already been dating other women. He even bought himself a sharp new convertible. The car plus his athletic good looks and his growing reputation as a broadcaster made him very popular in Des Moines. He was considered charming and handsome, but he was humble and modest about his accomplishments. In one-on-one conversations, he always left people feeling that he was deeply interested in them and their lives.

He also became a reserve officer in the Fourteenth Cavalry Regiment stationed at Camp Dodge in Des Moines. He had loved horses as a child but never had much chance to ride them. With the cavalry, he could ride as much as he wanted and get training in how to handle horses.

One of the most unusual aspects of his radio job was a requirement that he broadcast play-by-play

25

rundowns on Chicago Cubs and White Sox games. Reagan was in a studio in Des Moines, hundreds of miles from the games, and got the plays via telegraph messages from Chicago, so he had to provide colorful commentary on games he could not even see. He would talk about players stepping out of the batter's box to wipe their hands on their clothes and catchers giving signs to pitchers—details he simply made up. He also played a record of audience applause after good plays. Most of the audience knew what he was doing; in the early days of radio it was not only considered acceptable but was expected.

One summer afternoon Reagan was running through a Cubs game as usual when a message was passed to him: the telegraph wire had gone dead. Dutch's talent for storytelling, an ability he may have inherited from his Irish father, stood him in good stead. For almost seven minutes he stayed on the air giving a colorful rundown on how the batter kept fouling off pitches from Dizzy Dean.

Although friends in Des Moines considered him someone who might bend the truth a bit, as he did in these broadcasts, he was also known for his upstanding behavior. He visited bars and dances with friends but rarely drank; he still believed strongly in God and had patriotic faith in his country. Like his father, he was an ardent Democrat, but he had reservations about the effectiveness of the welfare system. Welfare, he believed, might be needed to help people for a while, but in the end people could gain financial security and self-esteem only through hard work.

Although he had to send a good part of his salary home because his father had had a heart attack and could no longer work, Reagan was moving smoothly ahead in his career. In fact, after a few years on the radio, Dutch Reagan was a celebrity in Des Moines, where he gave speeches at sports banquets and sometimes wrote newspaper columns. But he had never given up his old dream of going to Hollywood to become a movie star, and he soon devised a plan to break into films.

In the spring of 1937 Reagan convinced the station managers that he should go to Catalina Island, off the coast of southern California, to cover spring training with the Chicago Cubs. He would gather good material, he told his bosses, to use in his made-up telegraph-wire broadcasts. Furthermore, he said, if the station paid for the trip, he would use his own vacation time to cover the story. The station executives agreed to send him.

On his way to Catalina, Reagan paid a few calls in Hollywood. One stop was to see a young singer who had once worked for WHO. She got him an appointment with an agent.

As Reagan sat across the desk from the man, he outlined his background in college dramatics and in broadcasting. Suddenly the agent picked up the phone and dialed a casting director for Warner Brothers. "Max," he told the man on the other end of the line, "I have another Robert Taylor sitting in my office."[4]

That was an exaggeration: Robert Taylor was one of Hollywood's brightest leading men. But Warner Brothers agreed to give Reagan a screen test. A few days later Reagan acted on camera in a short scene. He and a young starlet, June Travis, spoke a few lines from a play that was later filmed as a movie with Cary Grant as the star. After seeing the brief test, the casting director, Max Arnow, decided that he liked Reagan's speaking voice. Reagan was asked to stay in Los Angeles until the studio's head, Jack Warner, had seen his film clip. But Reagan had to be on the train the next day, he told the studio people. He had a job in Des Moines, and baseball season was starting. All the way home, he regretted his decision, thinking that he had perhaps missed an opportunity by not staying in L.A. a little longer. A few days later he was back at WHO, where he told stories about Hollywood and joked with friends about his screen test. It had been fun, but he was ready to forget all about movies and stardom.

Then a telegram was delivered: "Warners offers contract seven years, one year's option, starting at $200 a week. What shall I do? Meiklejohn Agency."

Reagan gave a wild yell that was heard throughout the office. He was going to Hollywood to pursue his dream of a successful acting career. He was destined for movie stardom—or so he thought.

CHAPTER THREE
TROUBLE AT HOME AND ABROAD

In May 1937, Reagan drove his Nash convertible West to Los Angeles. When he got to Warner Brothers Studio in Burbank, he found out that the people there were eager for him to get to work.

The contract that had sounded so wonderful when he heard about it back in Iowa turned out to have some catches to it. True, it was a seven-year contract, but every six months Warner Brothers could decide whether it wanted to keep him. He would be paid $200 a week, but he was only guaranteed nineteen weeks of work out of every twenty-six. If he made money by appearing on radio or in advertising, he had to turn it over to the studio. He could not quit and go to another studio.

Furthermore, he found out that Warner, like most studios, made two kinds of films: A movies, which had big budgets, long shooting schedules, and big stars; and B movies, which had small budgets, were produced in three or four weeks, and starred actors no one had ever heard of—actors like Ronald Reagan. Yet Reagan was thrilled to be in Hollywood and was awed by the huge studio and the people who milled around its soundstages, offices, wardrobe rooms, and warehouses.

Reagan was twenty-six years old, slim, tall, and

handsome, with the athletic build he had had in college. Very quickly he was taken in hand by wardrobe people and makeup artists who changed his hairstyle and dabbed makeup on the bridge of his nose. They did not try to change his name—Ronald Reagan sounded just fine—but he couldn't call himself Dutch anymore. Also, he could not wear glasses on camera; so at first everything was a fuzzy blur as he acted out scenes. Later he wore the earliest types of contact lenses, big disks that covered the entire eye and felt very hard and rigid.

A few days after he arrived, he was rushed onto the set of his first film, *Love Is on the Air.* Reagan played the lead role of Andy McLeod, a radio newscaster demoted by his boss to kiddie show host until he came up with a big crime story. Then he was rushed off to California's Monterey peninsula to film *Sergeant Murphy,* about a cavalry officer devoted to a horse that ends up winning a big race. After that, it was one B movie after another with occasional small parts in A films. In all, he made eight pictures during his first eleven months in Hollywood. "I was proud of some of the B pictures we made," he said, "but a lot of them were pretty poor. They were movies the studio didn't want good, they wanted 'em Thursday."[1]

He lived a lonely bachelor life in a Hollywood apartment for those first few months and met few people except those he worked with. Sometimes he dated women he met on the set, but for the most part he socialized very little and missed his friends from back in Des Moines.

In his spare time he read a lot and picked up a huge assortment of opinions and facts and figures on politics and the economy. According to one actor, Larry Williams, who made five films with Reagan: "Ron had the dope on just about everything: this quarter's up-or-down figures on the gross national product growth, V. I. Lenin's grandfather's occupation, all history's baseball pitchers' ERAs and so on."[2]

Six months rolled by quickly, and Reagan grew worried that his career in films might be over. But the studio picked up his option for another six months and raised his salary to $250 a week for the weeks he worked. He felt confident enough about his future movie career to send for his parents. At first they lived in West Hollywood. Eventually, though, he bought them a house; it was small, but it was the nicest home they had ever had. Some of Reagan's fraternity brothers from college moved out west to Hollywood, too, in hopes of making a name for themselves in the movies like him. They got nowhere, but for a few months they lived in his apartment while they hunted jobs. He happily drove them around Hollywood on sight-seeing trips.

After a full year as an actor, however, Reagan's career seemed to be sputtering. The goal for any actor in B films, of course, was to become popular enough with film directors and fans so that he could move up to the A level. But fan mail did not come flooding in.

Of course, he was always hardworking and cooperative with directors. He showed up on time for work and always memorized his lines. Still he did not seem to worry about acting technique or improving his skills. "I became the Errol Flynn of the B's," Reagan said. "I was as brave as Errol but in low-budget pictures."[3]

There was one rough-and-tumble action scene after another in his films: he fought in prisons, he fought in a dirigible that had gone down at sea, he fought in an airplane with a trapdoor. A bottle was even shot out of his hand with a slingshot. It was all lively and fun but not very artistic.

Then in 1938 he was cast in a slightly better

film, *Brother Rat,* based on a Broadway play about a military school. Reagan played one of three cadets at the school. What was special about the film was that it featured a young actress, Jane Wyman, who was also struggling her way through B pictures. The two were attracted to each other, but Reagan was hesitant because Wyman was still getting a divorce from her first husband, a clothing company executive. Reagan's straitlaced religious background gave him doubts about dating a woman who was still married—and even one who was divorced.

But during filming of a sequel, *Brother Rat and a Baby,* Wyman and Reagan began seeing each other steadily. They went golfing, played tennis, and went ice-skating. Jane was falling in love, but Reagan seemed to have trouble expressing his feelings for her. Like Reagan, Wyman had had something of a tough childhood. Her birth mother had given her up for adoption when she was five years old. She was then raised by a strict German couple. As a teen she had dreamed about becoming an actress. She even dropped out of high school in 1932 to earn money for dancing lessons. But although Reagan handled his family problems by remaining even-tempered, totally in control of his emotions, Wyman could be moody and mercurial.

Reagan's self-control meant that their romance remained lukewarm for a while. When Wyman was hospitalized for a stomach problem, Reagan sent her a bouquet with the coldly worded message, "Get well soon, Ronald Reagan."[4] Was he her boyfriend, or wasn't he? she wondered. By the time Reagan came to visit her at the hospital, she was so angry she refused to see him. But he was serious about their relationship. He persisted until she saw him again. Soon after that they became engaged, and Wyman wore a huge amethyst engagement ring.

Reagan in a scene from the 1938 movie *Brother Rat* with Jane Wyman and Wayne Morris. It was on the set of this film that Reagan first met Wyman, who would later become his wife.

On January 26, 1940, they were married at the Wee Kirk O'Heather Church in Glendale in a small wedding with only Reagan's parents and a few other relatives and friends present. Wyman wore a pale blue satin dress and carried a mink muff covered with orchids. To movie fans, it seemed like a fairy tale, with Reagan, the shining knight on a white horse, rescuing the divorced Hollywood princess from her troubled past.

After their marriage, Reagan served on the board of the Screen Actors Guild, a union for actors, to which both he and Wyman belonged. He also began to meet many influential people, including prominent Republicans. Reagan, however, remained a staunch Democrat and a supporter of Franklin Delano Roosevelt.

He also got his first major role in an A movie. For some time, he had thought that the life of Notre Dame football star, George Gipp, who had died while attending the school, would make a good movie. Reagan had even considered writing his own screenplay for the project. Then one day he spotted a newspaper article that said that Warner was planning a film about the life of Knute Rockne, the Notre Dame football coach who had coached George Gipp. Pat O'Brien, a friend of Reagan's, was going to play Rockne, and several actors were in the running for the part of Gipp.

When Reagan asked to audition for the role, the

Reagan demonstrates his straight-arm technique in a promotional shot for the 1940 movie *Knute Rockne—All American*, in which he played the role of George Gipp, the Notre Dame football legend.

producer told him he didn't look big enough to be a football player. "You mean Gipp has to weigh about two hundred pounds?" he asked. "Would it surprise you that I'm five pounds heavier than George Gipp was when he played at Notre Dame?"[5]

He even rushed home to get a photo of himself in his college football uniform to show to the producer. The next day he had his screen test for the part, and the day after that, he had the role. Although Gipp was not on screen very much during the film, his role included a lot of action and an emotional death scene that allowed an actor to show off his talent.

In that death scene Reagan talks to Rockne and says a few lines that have become very famous: "Some day when things are tough and the breaks are going against the boys, ask them to go in there and win one for the Gipper."[6]

It was a moving speech that often brought tears to the eyes of those who watched it. After that film, Reagan was often called "the Gipper."

Reagan's performance impressed studio officials, and they began to cast him in better pictures. Shortly after the making of the Rockne film, Reagan and Wyman had their first child, Maureen, born on January 4, 1941. The little family soon moved from an apartment into a brand-new eight-room house.

Things seemed to be looking up for Ronald Reagan. The only sad note was that in May 1941, his father, Jack, died at age fifty-eight. Jack had long since given up drinking and had taken a small job at Warner Brothers where he handled his son's fan mail. The making of *Knute Rockne, All American* had made him especially proud of his son.

After that film, Reagan's acting career peaked with the making of *Kings Row*, a film shot in the summer of 1941. Reagan played Drake McHugh, a rich young man living in a small town at the turn of the century. First Drake loses all his money; then he gets into an accident and his legs are cut off by a doctor who is angry that Drake is in love with his daughter.

For days Reagan worried about how to play a crucial scene in which he wakes up in bed after the amputation and reacts to the surgery. When he reached the movie set that day he had to lie down in a bed rigged so that his legs fit into part of the mattress. As he lay there, he really felt as if his legs had been cut off. When the director yelled, "Action," Reagan yelled, "Where is the rest of me?" while he reached for his missing legs with his hands.[7]

The scene had turned out perfectly, the director decided; there was no reshooting. In fact, Reagan had done so well that there were rumors he would be nominated for an Oscar for his performance. That didn't happen, but still Warner was expecting to use Reagan in bigger and better films. The studio offered him a new contract with a big pay raise.

The only problem was that World War II got in the way of Reagan's career. He had joined the army reserves, and soon he was ordered into active service. Because of his poor eyesight, he could not serve in combat. So he was assigned to an air force intelligence unit to make training films and documentaries. The so-called First Motion Picture Unit was based at the Hal Roach Studios in Culver City, which had been nicknamed Fort Roach. Although at first Reagan spent most of the week at Fort Roach, he went home on weekends. Later he was even allowed to go home every night. Strangely enough, some of the fan magazines ran stories about him while he was in the service that sounded as if he were thousands of miles away from his wife and child.

Reagan and Jane Wyman with their daughter, Maureen Elizabeth, in 1946. The couple were divorced in June 1949.

At first he worked as a military personnel officer, but later he acted in films produced at the fort. One was a musical, *This Is the Army,* based on a Broadway play, in which he played the romantic lead. Both military people and civilians acted in the film, but the military actors like Reagan received no salary other than service pay.

Reagan worked hard during the war, eventually being promoted to the rank of captain. His wife, Jane, who bore the burden of supporting the family, made movie after movie, most of them very forgettable films. Her work often took her away from her daughter, but in spite of that, the couple decided they wanted another child. In March 1945 they adopted a baby boy, Michael. They issued a statement saying that they were adopting because they felt so many children already in the world needed loving homes.

Despite their children, however, the Reagans were growing apart. At war's end, Reagan left the service for Warner Brothers and began drawing his high salary again; but he had no movies to work in. Meanwhile, Jane Wyman was getting the kinds of roles she had longed for. MGM had chosen her to play the mother in *The Yearling,* based on the best-selling novel by Marjorie Kinnan Rawlings.

Once again Reagan's career in films seemed shaky, and suddenly his marriage seemed shaky as well.

CHAPTER FOUR
SCREEN IDLE

It wasn't until nine months after leaving the military that Reagan made *Stallion Road,* about life on a horse ranch. He loved making the movie and did all his own riding, but it was a forgettable film. Some critics even said that the horses outshone the actors. Reagan continued to get movie roles, but none of the films he appeared in achieved the same success as *Knute Rockne* and *Kings Row.* With each movie failure he found new roles harder and harder to come by.

Reagan suddenly had a lot of extra time on his hands, but he did not remain idle. Having been interested in politics for some time, he decided to get involved in Hollywood politics. He was still a staunch liberal and had been very upset by the death of President Franklin Roosevelt during World War II. He remained a member of the board of the Screen Actors Guild, but he also joined some very liberal organizations such as the American Veterans Committee and the Hollywood Independent Citizens Committee of Arts, Sciences and Professions. Later he quit these two groups after deciding that they had been infiltrated by Communists.

In 1946 a small group of stagehands went on strike and asked the guild members to support them by not crossing the picket lines at movie sets. At about this time Reagan was elected president of the guild, and he urged the board and members not to go on strike as well. He believed it was purely a fight between two stagehand groups over which group would control a production union. There were daily fights outside the studio gates when actors crossed the picket lines. Reagan contended that Communists were behind the violence. Reagan's growing fear of communism seemed exaggerated, almost like a movie plot. It led him to give the FBI the names of Screen Actors Guild members suspected of being Communists. He also testified in October 1947 before the House Un-American Activities Committee about liberal groups in Hollywood. But the House committee did not ask Reagan to give names of people he thought were Communists. Reagan also went along with the studios in their decision to deny jobs to actors who refused to cooperate with the Un-American Activities Committee. While Reagan was guild president, the group adopted a loyalty oath in which new members had to swear allegiance to the United States. In all this, Reagan was like many Americans who grew fearful after World War II about the growing influence of the Communist Soviet Union in Europe. Many feared that Communists might infiltrate and take over the United States. But in the process, many innocent people lost their jobs, their friends, and even their families as a result of being labeled Communists. Reagan contended that if he and others had not been vigilant, Communists could have taken over the film business. "I knew from firsthand experience how Communists used lies, deceit, violence or any other tactics that suited them to advance the cause of Soviet expansionism," he said later.[1]

As president of the Screen Actors Guild, Reagan

Reagan, head of the Screen Actors Guild, testifies before the House Un-American Activities Committee. In 1947 he helped the committee investigate alleged Communist activities among the guild membership.

was active in the group's negotiations with film producers. His film career might not have been flourishing, but his interest in politics was growing as was his ability to handle people and make speeches. Then, in 1946, Reagan's wife, Jane Wyman, won an important film role as a young deaf-mute woman in *Johnny Belinda*. Wyman plunged into preparing for the role. She went to a school for deaf-mutes and learned to read lips. She lost weight and became almost obsessed with the part. Eventually she would win an Oscar for her convincing portrayal.

But her husband did not seem to understand her need to pour herself into the role. Gossip columnists began to write about the troubles Reagan and Wyman were having, many of them blaming her. Feeling an increasing distance between herself and her husband, Wyman began to spend time with Lew Ayres, one of her costars in *Johnny Belinda*.

Finally, in early 1948, Reagan and Wyman separated. They tried a couple of times to get back together, but Wyman filed suit for divorce in June. "In recent months," she told the divorce judge, "my husband and I engaged in continual arguments on his political views."[2] He had demanded that she go to political meetings with him, she said, but they did not share the same politics.

Reagan did not contest the divorce, but he grieved deeply for his lost marriage. For some time he did not date other women, although by Hollywood standards he was considered a very eligible bachelor. He continued to act in mediocre films and to be active in Hollywood politics. Most of his spare time he spent visiting his mother and his children or working with his horses on a small ranch in which he had a part-interest.

As time passed, he began to date other women, mostly actresses, and in the fall of 1949 he met a young actress, Nancy Davis, whom he started dating steadily. The story she told about their meeting was that she had been reading a Hollywood newspaper and had seen her name on a list of Communist sympathizers. In a panic, she contacted a director friend who knew Ronald Reagan, the guild president. At Nancy's request, Reagan called her to talk about how to clear her name.

Others in Hollywood, however, contend that the two met first at a dinner party. Whatever the circumstances, by spring 1950, Reagan and Nancy Davis were seeing each other steadily, although Reagan still dated other women and sometimes saw his ex-wife. Often Reagan and Nancy double-dated with their friends, actor Bill Holden and his wife, Ardis. After Reagan and Nancy had dated for about two years, he asked her to marry him. She later said that they would probably have married sooner had he not felt torn about his broken marriage to Wyman. "Like most of his generation, he had been brought up to believe that you married once, and that was it," she said.[3]

Nancy Davis was the daughter of an actress, Edith Luckett, who had married a Chicago neurosurgeon, Loyal Davis. Both Loyal and Edith had been married before. Nancy was the daughter of Edith's first husband, but Loyal Davis adopted Nancy when he married her mother. Nancy had gone to Smith College and then decided to pursue an acting career. Through her mother's connections she got small parts in some Broadway plays and eventually a Hollywood contract.

When she met Reagan, Davis had been in only a few movies. She was twenty-eight years old, and her career in films was sputtering. Although Reagan did not seem immediately ready to make a commitment to her, she seemed ready to give up films for him. She went to his political meetings, she helped him entertain his children, she painted fences on his ranch. While his long political speeches had bored Jane Wyman, Nancy loved to listen to him spin stories for hours.

They were married on March 4, 1952, at the Little Brown Church in the Valley. It was a simple ceremony, and very few guests were in attendance. Ardis Holden was the matron of honor and Bill Holden was the best man. Nancy was pregnant with the couple's first child.

Soon the newlyweds bought a home in Pacific Palisades, a comfortable seven-room house, but not nearly as extravagant as one might expect for two Hollywood actors. The fact was that Reagan's career had taken a nosedive. He was being offered films of low quality. One of his last movies before he remarried had been *Bedtime for Bonzo,* in which he played a college professor with a chimpanzee for a close friend.

Both Ronald and Nancy had agreed that he had to turn down poor scripts, but very few good ones were sent to him to consider. This was because most studio executives felt that Reagan, now forty-four years old, had never been an outstanding actor. He had been in forty-five films; if he hadn't become a star by now, he probably never would.

For several months Reagan did television guest spots, but in the end he went back to making inferior films. After all, his family was growing. His daughter, Patricia Ann Reagan, was born on October 22, 1952. Nancy wanted to stay home to be a full-time wife and mother, but she, too, had to contribute to the family income. Shortly after Patti was born, she acted in a low-budget film, *Donovan's Brain.* Her willingness to work was typical of how fiercely loyal to Reagan Nancy could be. "Nancy's his best friend," said a future aide to Reagan.[4]

Reagan even put together a Las Vegas nightclub

Reagan and Nancy Davis, whom he met in 1949, were married on March 4, 1952. This photo was taken of the couple on their honeymoon, in Phoenix, Arizona.

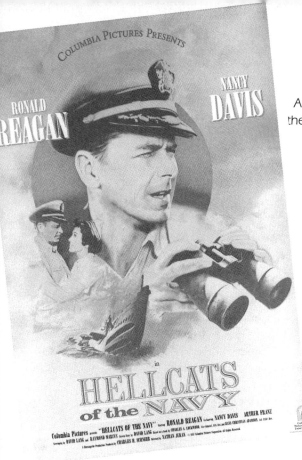

A promotional poster for the 1957 potboiler *Hellcats of the Navy*, in which Reagan played a courageous World War II submarine commander in the South Pacific. The movie also starred Reagan's wife, Nancy.

As movie roles became difficult to find, Reagan took jobs he normally would have turned down and got involved in politics. Here he performs as a singing waiter as part of his act during a two-week Las Vegas engagement in February 1954.

act. He told jokes, did a vaudeville routine, and recited a poem about an actor's life. The performance was third-rate, and he knew it. He never played Las Vegas again.

Even his political work had slowed down. He contended that Hollywood left-wingers were angry at him for his strong stand against communism. He had also been involved in negotiations with Music Corporation of America, or MCA, a talent agency, under which the Screen Actors Guild allowed MCA to produce television shows. This meant that MCA could represent actors and also hire them for jobs—a situation that seemed like a conflict of interest. Because Reagan himself was a client of MCA, other actors began to question his leadership.

Possibly because of these conflicts, but also because he was tired of the work, Reagan resigned as guild president. He had served as its chief officer for six years. Clearly he had to find a new direction for his life, but what would it be?

CHAPTER FIVE
BEARING RIGHT

In his suit and tie, Reagan looked ready to attend a Hollywood banquet rather than to visit a factory. As he strolled among waiting lines of employees at a General Electric turbine plant in New York State, workers put their work aside. Everyone wanted to chat with the visiting film actor, faded though his star might be. They wanted an autograph from this man with the big smile, who acted like a new neighbor eager to please them.

The warmth and small talk felt good to Reagan, who had gone through a discouraging year and a half. He and Nancy had been running low on money, and he had been offered few film roles. Those that came his way were low-budget, low-quality movies. Maybe his Hollywood career was over. One night he came home feeling particularly depressed after attending a meeting covered by the press. He told Nancy that he had overheard someone joke, "Well, at last Ronald Reagan is having his picture taken."[1]

Then in 1954, the General Electric Company asked Reagan to serve as host of its Sunday night television program. Each week a different cast would play out a different drama on the show, and Reagan would introduce the telecast. Sometimes he would act in the plays, too. Like most Hollywood actors, fearful of overexposure, Reagan had generally turned down television offers. But he was running out of options, and he liked this job because he did not have to play the same character week after week, as did most actors in television series. In addition to his television performances, GE wanted him to travel regularly to its plants around the country as a way of bringing employees closer together. At first, as in that visit to the New York factory, Reagan just walked around to chat with employees one-on-one. Then he started giving little speeches to small groups, talking about the movie business and answering questions.

Pretty soon he started explaining his philosophy of life, talking to workers "about the pride of giving and the importance of doing things without waiting for the government to do it for you," as he later said.[2] In his speeches he gave down-to-earth, homespun all-American advice that suited GE just fine.

Reagan visited all 139 GE plants in the next eight years. He estimated that he shook hands with 250,000 workers. GE managers liked him so much that they asked him to speak to local clubs and service groups. There he talked about the need for individuals to make it on their own and the need to keep government from interfering too much in Americans' daily lives. Most of those in the audience, many of them businessmen, agreed completely. They complained, Reagan said, about how government bureaucrats pushed them around. "I heard it so often," he said, "that after a while I became convinced that some of our fundamental freedoms were in jeopardy."[3]

Reagan, the onetime supporter of Franklin Delano Roosevelt's New Deal, was sounding more and more like a conservative Republican as he attacked big government spending and rules. More and more, too, his speeches sounded like those of a politician on the campaign trail. Some audience members even urged him to run for governor or senator as they shook his hand.

Hollywood wasn't out of his blood yet, though. In 1956, Reagan and Nancy made a film together. Called *Hellcats of the Navy,* it was partly filmed on a submarine docked in San Diego. Then Nancy retired from acting, and in 1958 their son, Ronald Prescott, was born.

Reagan returned to serve another term as president of the Screen Actors Guild and led the group in its first major strike. The strike succeeded; producers agreed to pay actors a share of the money made from selling films to television. Reagan may have hurt his film career with this labor activity, but still, he was becoming a wealthy man. After all, General Electric was paying him $150,000 a year. He and Nancy soon built a dream house overlooking the ocean in Pacific Palisades. They also bought a 350-acre ranch in the Santa Monica Mountains north of Los Angeles.

Although Reagan endorsed Republican candidates, including Richard Nixon, he remained a registered Democrat. Steadily, though, his views became more conservative. Nancy may have played a role in this, or perhaps her stepfather, Loyal Davis, a conservative Republican, influenced Reagan, who greatly admired this successful surgeon as he had never admired his own father.

Then in 1962, Reagan was campaigning again for Nixon who was running for governor against the California incumbent, Edmund G. Brown Sr. As Reagan tells it, he was speaking at a party when a woman in the audience asked if he was a registered Republican. Reagan said he wasn't, but he planned to change his party soon. "I'm a registrar," the woman said, walking up to hand him the proper form. Reagan signed it and went on with his speech.[4] He had officially joined the Republicans.

At about this time, Reagan's job with GE fell apart. He claimed it was because of a change in management at the company. The new managers, he said, had asked him to cut out the political messages and stick to selling products, and Reagan refused. Others say GE was worried because Reagan had run into trouble with the government over a possible conflict of interest. Supposedly he had gotten his GE job through MCA, the company that won special favors from the Screen Actors Guild while he was serving as guild president. Government investigators wanted to know how he could represent the actors and still accept a job from a company with which he was negotiating. Nothing ever came of the investigation, but for whatever reason, *The GE Theater* was canceled.

Once again Reagan was out of work, but this time he was in better shape financially. In 1964 he made his last film, *The Killers,* based on an Ernest Hemingway story. He played a villain for the first time and seemed uncomfortable with the role. After that he appeared as a guest star on television and served as host of another program, *Death Valley Days,* a Western dramatic series. He also found time for politics and traveled on behalf of the Republican Party.

Then, in the summer of 1964, the Republicans picked a staunch conservative, Arizona senator Barry Goldwater, as their presidential candidate. Reagan stood squarely behind Goldwater even though the candidate and his right-wing supporters threatened to split the party ideologically.

Goldwater's campaign sputtered from the start. Many Americans feared he would cut back programs like Social Security, launched as part of the Roosevelt administration's New Deal. They were also afraid he might cause new conflicts with the Soviet Union and lead the nation into nuclear war. Many usually devoted Republicans even decided to vote for the Democratic incumbent president, Lyndon B. Johnson.

But while other Republicans backed away, Reagan appeared at many fund-raisers for Goldwater in California and across the nation. After speaking at one successful dinner in Los Angeles, Reagan was approached by influential California Republicans. Would he give the same speech for Goldwater on national television if they bought airtime?

Reagan readily agreed, but some on Goldwater's staff had doubts. Reagan's speech had little to say about Goldwater, and besides, they said, if television time was available, maybe Goldwater should use it. But Goldwater agreed to the plan, and on October 27, 1964, Reagan gave what he later called one of the most important speeches of his career. It repeated themes he had stressed for years—the burden of taxes and the need for the people to control government rather than for government to control the people. He talked about individual freedom: "You and I are told increasingly that we have to choose between a left or right, but I would like to suggest that there is no such thing as a left or right. There is only an up or down—up to man's age-old dream—the ultimate in individual freedom consistent with law and order—or down to the ant heap of totalitarianism."[5]

His closing words borrowed liberally from Winston Churchill, Franklin Roosevelt, and Abraham Lincoln: "You and I have a rendezvous with destiny. We will preserve for our children this, the last best hope of man on earth, or we will sentence them to take the last step into a thousand years of darkness."[6]

Reagan talked only a little bit about Goldwater, but still calls flooded in to the Goldwater-for-president headquarters from people who wanted to pledge money and support. Those who saw Reagan as a possible candidate were very impressed. But Goldwater lost badly: Johnson won with the largest percentage of the popular vote, 61.1, that had ever been recorded.

Republicans lost more than the presidency that year. Democrats also won Republican seats in the House of Representatives and the Senate, and Republicans were losers in state and local races, including California. After the election, the Republicans controlled only seven of the fifty state legislatures and seventeen governorships. The nation had completely rejected Goldwater's conservative message and had chosen a liberal course. It seemed like a poor time for a conservative Republican like Reagan to get interested in politics.

But after the election, several wealthy Republicans visited Reagan to press him to run for governor of California. "I said that I felt that we had to start rebuilding, and if he would, we were committed to see that he got the necessary funds and the organization to run," said Holmes Tuttle, a Beverly Hills car dealer.[7]

Reagan claimed later that he was stunned by their plan. "I'm an actor, not a politician," he said he told them. "I'm in show business."[8]

But the proposal could not have been a complete surprise to Reagan; for years people had been urging him to run for one office or another, and he had discussed the idea before. After a month, Reagan called Tuttle to say he wanted to give politics a try

Reagan, the Republican candidate for governor of California in 1966, campaigns in Los Angeles. Although a Democrat in his youth, Reagan had moved significantly to the right before making a bid for governor.

but would put out some feelers first. According to Reagan, he gave speeches around the state to see what the public thought of him. Finally, on January 4, 1966, he announced he was running for governor of California.

First Reagan had to face another Republican to win the nomination. His opponent was George Christopher, a former mayor of San Francisco who ran as a moderate and tried to play up Reagan's reputation as a right-wing conservative. Christopher was a poor campaigner and was not well known in southern California. Reagan beat him by a better than two-to-one margin and carried fifty-three of the fifty-eight counties in the state.

Next, Reagan took on Edmund G. Brown, Sr., the incumbent Democratic governor who had already soundly beaten the former presidential candidate, Richard Nixon, in 1962. Brown was delighted to face Reagan in the race. On one hand, he could portray Reagan as an extreme right-winger, a friend of Goldwater. On the other hand, he could point out that Reagan was an actor, a resident of Tinsel Town, a speaker who might sound impressive and look good but who belonged on screen, not in the governor's chair.

Meanwhile, Reagan assembled a top-flight team of campaign advisers, including a political consulting team. He hired an aggressive communications director, Lyn Nofziger, a man who would work for him for many years after that. A pair of college professors joined the campaign to advise Reagan on issues and policies.

Reagan concentrated his campaign in southern California, which was more densely populated than the north. He focused especially on the suburbs where white middle-class voters were upset at the political unrest and anti-Vietnam War protests on campuses of state colleges and universities. While the outspoken Goldwater had irritated middle-of-the-road Republicans, the more personable Reagan attracted them, even though he actually shared many of Goldwater's ideas.

Reagan's easygoing charm and folksy western-style humor was popular even with blue-collar workers, most of whom were strong Democrats at the time. After all, he could point out that he had led the Screen Actors Guild in a strike. Union leaders endorsed Brown, but the rank and file liked Reagan.

Meanwhile, the incumbent Brown was in deep trouble. He had lost the support of many liberals because he had backed President Lyndon Johnson's policies on Vietnam. Brown's support in the black community had also slipped because blacks did not believe he had given them enough economic help. Then, in September 1966, blacks rioted in the Hunters Point and Bayview sections of San Francisco after a white policeman shot and killed a black teenager who was fleeing police. Although Brown was not responsible for the looting and violence, voters viewed the incident as symbolic of his administration's inability to keep the peace.

Brown hammered away at Reagan for being an actor rather than a man who was prepared to govern. He also accused Reagan of being a member of the John Birch Society, a group on the right-wing fringe with which Reagan was, in fact, not involved.

On election night the race seemed to be over before it had started. Reagan and his wife were driving to what they hoped would be a victory party at the Century Plaza Hotel in Los Angeles when they heard on the radio that Reagan had won. "It can't be over," Nancy Reagan said. "We're not at the party yet."[9]

It was a Reagan landslide: he had won by a margin of almost a million votes. The people of California had elected a new governor.

With his wife, Nancy, at his side, Reagan addresses
the crowd after being sworn in as California's thirty-
third governor on January 3, 1967, in Sacramento.
He won the election by a landslide.

CHAPTER SIX
MR. GOVERNOR

At midnight on January 3, 1967, Reagan, his family, and friends filed into the shadow-filled rotunda of the California Capitol building. Thirty-two television cameras focused on a platform built just for this occasion: the swearing in of the governor of California. After a chaplain gave the oath of office to Reagan, the new governor stepped up to the microphone. "Well, Murph," Reagan joked, looking at his friend George Murphy, U.S. senator from California and also a former actor, "here we are again on the late, late show."[1]

The swearing in was marked by drama and controversy, as much of Reagan's tenure as governor would be. After all, the official inauguration would not be held for two days, so why not delay the swearing-in ceremony until then? Nancy claimed her husband wanted to be sworn in early to stop the outgoing governor from appointing more Democratic judges. Others say no. "No governor in the history of California had ever chosen to take the oath of office in the middle of the night, but the Reagans were acting on advice from an astrologer, who said that this was the most propitious time," said a biographer of Nancy Reagan.[2] Over the years, many of Reagan's staff claimed Nancy set her husband's schedule based on the advice of an astrologer.

In his formal inaugural speech later that week, Reagan focused on two areas. He wanted to end the violence on California campuses, he said. And he promised "to squeeze and cut and trim" to solve the state's financial problems, which included a $194 million deficit.[3]

Reagan set a temporary freeze on hiring and appointed a team of business executives to see where cuts could be made. The cutting and slashing began, but in many cases some of the spending had to be restored because it was impossible to do without the programs. In other cases, federal or state laws made it impossible to cut the programs back. Cutting the budget was turning out to be a tougher job than Reagan had realized.

Although Reagan had promised to keep politics out of the process when he appointed new people to public office, most of the jobs went to Republicans, many of them picked by his so-called kitchen cabinet of wealthy advisers—people who had donated heavily to his campaign. This group was already planning for Reagan to run for president in 1968 and quietly opened a presidential campaign office in San Francisco.

The appointment process went fairly slowly—after all, Reagan and his advisers had little experience in government until then. Among those who joined the Reagan team in Sacramento were many men who stayed with him for years to come: Edwin Meese III became his personal executive assistant; Caspar Weinberger became finance director; Michael Deaver became assistant executive secretary.

Reagan followed a hands-off management style. He liked to pick people who fit his political philosophy. Then he set policies and goals and let his staff work on the details. Most days he got to the office a little before nine and left a little before six. "I don't think a chief executive should peer constantly over

Governor Reagan and First Lady Nancy, with
their children, Ronald and Patti, pose for a family
portrait at their home.

the shoulders of the people who are in charge of a project and tell them every few minutes what to do," he said.[4]

Throughout his political career, Reagan continued to take this hands-off approach, and his detractors often criticized him for remaining so removed from the nuts and bolts of governing. Still, others argued that a certain distance between an elected government official and the day-to-day activities of his or her staff is natural and proper. Regardless, the hands-off style was the one Reagan preferred, and it became one of his trademarks.

Another Reagan trademark was his belief that government was too big and too expensive. In line with this belief, Governor Reagan sought to cut spending wherever possible. For example, he very much wanted to make cuts in the state welfare program. Millions of needy and disabled people received welfare payments, Reagan admitted. But he insisted that many able-bodied teenage, unwed mothers were getting aid just because they did not want to work. In the end, he managed to do very little during his first term other than to set up a task force to study the welfare system and the requirements a person had to meet in order to receive welfare payments.

At first, Reagan came up with a simple plan to reduce the state's budget deficit. He proposed cutting all expenses in every department by 10 percent, even if that department was already overworked and efficiently run. He submitted his first budget to the state legislature in 1967 on that basis. But two months later he was back with another budget that trimmed the cuts to 6 percent instead of 10 percent. Eventually he was forced to restore even more of those cuts so that the final budget was more than $5 billion in all.

One place in which Reagan did reduce spending

was mental health care. After all, he reasoned, the number of patients in state mental hospitals had been dropping steadily due to the use of new drugs and medical techniques. Meanwhile the number of staff had not dropped. In reality, though, the staffs in these hospitals had never been as large as they should have been. Furthermore, once the patients with fewer problems left the hospitals, only the tough cases, needing much more care, were left behind. Nonetheless, Reagan proposed cutting the mental health staff by 3,700 jobs. There was a firestorm of criticism, and the cutback was trimmed to 2,600 jobs, but still mental health care suffered many changes. Some of Reagan's advisers who had proposed the cuts later admitted that had been a bad idea.

In his first term, Reagan also took on the University of California. The university campuses, scattered across the state, had been rocked in the 1960s by violent student marches and sit-ins, some staged in protest against the Vietnam War, some sparked by dissatisfaction of various minority groups. As historian James MacGregor Burns writes, "Many students felt alienated by the intellectual assembly line of a huge impersonal 'multiversity' harnessed to the needs of large corporations and the Pentagon."[5]

But Reagan, who ironically enough had once led a student protest at his own college, refused to acknowledge that these protesting students had any justification for their unrest. During his campaign he had called the protesters "bums" and alleged that they indulged in "sexual orgies."[6] "The upheaval that shook so many of our campuses when I was governor wasn't a gallant or idealistic rebellion to right some wrongs," he contended. "It was violent anarchy."[7]

After taking office, he proposed slashing the university budget and forcing students to pay tuition for the first time. This was partly due to the need to balance the budget, but his foes condemned it as a move to punish students for their political views. University officials reacted to Reagan by threatening to freeze enrollments and close campuses. Reagan had to compromise. He held the line on rising costs at the university, and he forced the university president, Clark Kerr, to leave his job. But the university regents, the governing board for the system, refused to impose tuition. Actually that was a debatable point; California students already had to pay "fees," and those fees were raised so much that they equaled the tuition paid by students in other states.

Reagan also took on the unrest at the state colleges, California's other publicly funded system of higher education. After two presidents resigned at San Francisco State College, which had been rocked by political protests, Reagan appointed a new president, S. I. Hayakawa, a conservative professor who stood up to demonstrators. Hayakawa went on to be elected a senator from California on the Republican ticket.

Throughout both of Reagan's terms as governor, student unrest continued. Reagan even sent rifle-bearing National Guardsmen into Berkeley at one point to quell disturbances over People's Park, a park that students wanted to save from development by the university.

Under orders from Governor Reagan, members of the National Guard confront demonstrators at People's Park in Berkeley, California, in May 1969.

As time passed, it became clear that the state could not pay its bills without tax increases. For years, the previous governor, Edmund G. Brown Sr., had delayed raising taxes to avoid upsetting voters. But Reagan had to do so or bankrupt the state. To get a tax increase, Reagan had to work with the state legislature, which was controlled by Democrats. In particular, he had to persuade Jesse "Big Daddy" Unruh, Democratic speaker of the assembly and one of the most powerful men in the state. If Reagan could do this, he could show the nation as a whole what a strong and powerful governor he was.

Together the two came up with a $1 billion tax package that included higher income taxes as well as higher sales, bank and corporation, and cigarette and liquor taxes. However, the bill also cut back the burden of property taxes paid by homeowners. Reagan agreed to many of Unruh's ideas in return for Unruh giving up a plan to withhold income taxes from the paychecks of Californians.

Unruh, who planned to run for governor himself, believed that the tax bill would hurt Reagan's career, but in fact, Reagan's reputation was enhanced. Most voters tended to blame Brown's administration for the state's budget woes and the need for new taxes. In addition, Reagan had shown that he could wheel and deal with top politicians to get the job done.

Early in his first term, Reagan faced the question of abortion, an issue that would divide the entire nation for years to come. Previously, California state law had said an abortion could be performed only to save a woman's life. But some California legislators wanted to allow abortions in cases of rape and incest and when a pregnancy might hurt the mental or physical health of a mother. Reagan agreed to these changes despite opposition from the

Catholic church. He insisted he would not support the bill if abortions could be performed to prevent the birth of a deformed child—for example, one whose mother had been exposed to German measles. He said, "I cannot justify morally . . . the taking of the unborn life simply on the supposition that it is going to be less than a perfect human being."[8] Lawmakers agreed to Reagan's changes, and the bill moved ahead. Then Reagan changed his mind and threatened to veto the bill. He feared that the provision allowing an abortion to prevent the impairment of a mother's mental health would be used to justify aborting a deformed baby.

Both Republican and Democratic legislators were furious with him. How could Reagan wait until the last minute to make an excuse for not signing the bill? They then approved the bill by a huge margin, thus showing Reagan they might override his veto. So Reagan gave in and signed the bill. If he had refused, he might have caused a deep conflict with the Republican lawmakers whose help he needed later on.

Although Reagan had always preached that the state had to get tough on crime, he was troubled and uncertain early in his first term as the state prepared, for the first time in four years, to execute a condemned prisoner. The man who was ready to go to the gas chamber at San Quentin Prison in April 1967 was Aaron Mitchell, a thirty-seven-year-old black man who had killed a policeman during a robbery. Reagan reviewed the case but found no grounds for granting Mitchell his life other than opposition to the death penalty itself. The trouble was, Reagan had always endorsed the death penalty. The day before the execution, Reagan told reporters that if the public asks policemen to risk their lives, people have "an obligation to them to let them know that society will do whatever it can to minimize the danger of their occupations."[9] Still Reagan spent a troubled night pondering his decision while pickets against the death penalty marched outside his house.

After Mitchell's execution, another death-penalty case came before Reagan, but this prisoner had a record of brain damage, and Reagan used that as a reason to grant clemency and spare the man's life. Because of various court actions and delays, no more prisoners were executed in California for twenty-five years.

From the beginning of his career in politics, Nancy Reagan was a strong influence on her husband and his opinions, and sometimes her actions sparked public criticism. Many in Sacramento found her very hard to get to know and thought she was interested in entertaining Hollywood celebrities rather than politicians and their families.

Soon after the Reagans moved to Sacramento, she sparked an uproar involving the governor's mansion, a ramshackle Victorian house in downtown Sacramento that was built in 1877. On her first tour of the house, Nancy Reagan was horrified: "The place reminded me of a funeral parlor. When we moved in, there were purple velvet drapes in each room—so old that when we took them down, they practically crumbled in our hands."[10]

She insisted that the mansion was a fire hazard, too dangerous for their eight-year-old son, Ron. Their daughter, Patti, with whom Nancy had many conflicts throughout the years, was away at boarding school in Arizona.

One night when Reagan came home, Nancy told him she wouldn't live in the mansion any longer. His advisers told her she would ruin Reagan's career if she moved out. "I can't help it," she told them. "I can't fulfill my duties as the wife of the governor, and my responsibilities as a mother."[11]

So in April 1967 the Reagans moved to an English-style home in the suburbs of Sacramento. At first they paid rent for the house; later the home was sold to some of their friends, and the Reagans rented it from them. Eventually the old governor's mansion became a museum, and the legislature, at Reagan's suggestion, built a more luxurious home in the suburbs above the American River. But the next governor, Jerry Brown, son of Edmund G. Brown, refused to use it because he considered it outrageously expensive.

CHAPTER SEVEN
WHO, ME?

According to Ronald Reagan, early in 1968, when he had been governor of California for less than two years, several state Republican leaders asked him to put his name in as a presidential candidate on the California primary ballot in June. They figured that if Reagan ran as the favorite-son candidate from California, no other candidates would want to enter their names on the state ballot. Supposedly such a move would prevent the kinds of bloody battles in the party that had occurred during the 1964 election. His delegation to the convention, Reagan insisted, would include both party moderates and conservatives.

Actually, Reagan's supporters had dreamed about making him a presidential candidate from the moment he was first elected governor. He continued to insist publicly and privately that he was not a serious candidate, but gradually he too began to get interested in the idea of running for president, and he cooperated when his aides booked him on speaking tours in southern states where he would be most likely to pick up votes.

The other candidates in the presidential race were Richard Nixon, the former presidential candidate, whom many Republicans regarded as a loser;

George Romney, former governor of Michigan; and Nelson Rockefeller, governor of New York. Romney quickly dropped out of the race, and soon Nixon and Rockefeller were the leading contenders. Nixon, whose name was very familiar to Republican voters, continued to win primaries in one state after another. In most of these states, Reagan did not allow his name to appear on the ballot. In Oregon, where Reagan was a candidate, he was soundly beaten by Nixon. But there was always the chance that there might be a convention deadlock between Rockefeller and Nixon and that delegates might turn to Reagan as a compromise candidate.

After all, despite his political inexperience, Reagan was wonderful with audiences. Even while giving poorly written speeches, he managed to ad-lib little jokes, often at his own expense, that made audiences love him. "No matter how bad his stuff may be," said one television newsman, "he comes through as a hero."[1] When reporters tried to trip him up, they came out looking like the villains.

Reagan's victory in the California primary was a foregone conclusion; no other major candidates had entered. But even that triumph was overshadowed by a chilling tragedy in Los Angeles on election night. The Democratic primary winner, Robert F. Kennedy, was assassinated at his victory party by a deranged gunman. Soon Secret Service agents were sent to Sacramento to protect Reagan, just as they were sent to protect other possible presidential candidates.

When the Republican convention opened in Miami Beach in early August, Reagan still held on to a sizable number of delegate votes, but it was becoming clear that he didn't have a chance to take the nomination away from Nixon. Conservatives in the party approached him and asked him to withdraw from the race, but Reagan hesitated. All along he had said he wasn't a candidate, that he was just playing the favorite-son role to help prevent the party's nomination from falling to the wrong candidate. But at the last minute he announced that he was a candidate after all. It was something of a political blunder that showed he was not very realistic about Nixon's strength as a candidate.

That made no difference, however. There were no convention surprises. When the final vote was taken, Nixon won soundly. Reagan went to the podium and in a warm gesture urged that the vote be made unanimous for Nixon. "When Nixon was nominated, I was the most relieved person in the world," Reagan said. "I knew I wasn't ready to be president."[2]

Soon after the convention Reagan announced that he would run for a second term as governor. His opponent in that 1970 election was Jesse Unruh, the speaker of the California Assembly, the man he had worked with so closely on the tax bill.

Unruh had been a very powerful politician who had done much to reform the operations of the California legislature. But in the eyes of most voters, he seemed to be a wheeler-dealer who represented the worst in California politics. He could not seem to shed his "Big Daddy" nickname.

He tried to combat this by labeling Reagan the "tool of the rich," an actor closely allied with millionaires. But the label failed to stick. One blunder after another beset Unruh's campaign.

Reagan was a front-runner from the beginning and declined to hold any debates with the stumbling Unruh. Reagan won by a margin of 53 percent of the vote to Unruh's 45 percent.

During his campaign, Reagan had pledged to clean up the welfare system in California; the num-

Balloons are released in support of the candidacy of
Ronald Reagan at the 1968 Republican National
Convention in Miami, Florida. Reagan eventually
lost the nomination to Richard Nixon.

ber of poor Californians receiving money from the state had been increasing rapidly in the 1960s. "Public assistance should go to the needy and not the greedy," he had kept saying to voters as he argued that many of those on welfare did not deserve to be given the money and ought to get jobs and earn a salary.[3]

So as his second term began, Reagan focused on reforming the welfare system. In his first term he had muddled around when he talked about cost-cutting and trimming the budget—often taking action before he fully knew what he was doing.

But this time he was well prepared and had a careful plan worked out by a committee appointed to study welfare problems. If the numbers on the welfare rolls were not curbed soon, his staff told him, a huge tax increase might be needed. In 1963 there had been 375,000 California families receiving Aid to Families with Dependent Children. In 1970 there were more than 1.56 million.

Many states were beset by this same problem, and lots of them were starting to take drastic measures.

Reagan presented to the legislature seventy specific reforms for the welfare system. He waged a public campaign, complaining to the people of California that the Democratic-controlled legislature was blocking needed changes. The Democrats responded by accusing Reagan of trying to take money away from families who had been hurt by an economic recession.

For a while there was an impasse, and then the new speaker of the assembly, Bob Moretti, approached Reagan about a compromise. As Moretti told it, he told the governor, "I don't like you particularly and I know you don't like me, but we don't have to be in love to work together. If you're serious about doing some things, then let's sit down and start doing it."[4]

But according to Reagan, Moretti stomped in and said, "Stop those cards and letters!"

Then Reagan said he responded, "Let's put aside our personal feelings and jointly go to work and see what we can get done."[5]

After that, the two worked out a package of reforms that Reagan claimed cut expenditures by hundreds of millions of dollars. The package included antifraud measures that required more record-checking to make sure that welfare recipients were not cheating the government. A new residency rule required recipients to live in the state for a year before getting aid. At the same time, Reagan agreed to raise payments to families who were legitimately on welfare. There was also a work program that pushed those who did not have very young children to do public service jobs in return for the aid.

The welfare rolls did decline immediately, and within three years the number of dependent families dropped from 1.6 million to 1.3 million. Reagan took full credit for the decrease and was widely applauded across the nation.

Democrats insisted the decline would have happened anyway because the economy had improved and because more and more welfare mothers were having abortions instead of babies under the state's new liberalized abortion law.

In 1972, Reagan and Moretti put together a one-cent increase in the sales tax. They also used a state budget surplus to come up with $1 billion in property tax relief for homeowners and to improve the financing of local schools.

In all, Reagan claimed, in his two administrations as governor, he had rebated more than $5.7 billion to the public—a figure his critics say is exag-

Reagan, who was reelected governor in 1970, vowed to reduce state government spending during his second term. However, by the time he left office in 1974, the state's annual budget had increased by about $6 billion over his two terms.

gerated. But the booming state economy did make it possible for much of the budget surplus to be returned to taxpayers.

Reagan has always claimed that the rebates were in part the result of his ability to control spending in state government. The truth was, though, that the state budget more than doubled in size while he was governor, going from $4.6 billion to $10.2 billion a year. One reason the budget exploded was that the population of California had grown; another reason was inflation. Like all government leaders, Reagan had also found that it was very difficult to stop the bureaucracy from growing.

According to an aide to Unruh, Judson Clark, Reagan "did some important things, but not as much as he said he would do and not as much as he said he did."[6]

CHAPTER EIGHT
WOUNDED, NOT SLAIN

In his last year as governor, Reagan seemed confused about his future. He had been extremely popular in his home state, although the fortunes of his party were sinking nationwide. Should he retire to a ranch that he and Nancy had bought near Santa Barbara? He wasn't ready to stop working entirely, but he could enter the lecture circuit again and make a great deal of money. Should he run for another term as governor? No, he was tired of being governor and ready for a new job.

Could he run for another office—possibly senator or even president? His financial backers did not want to fund a senate race, but more and more people were considering Reagan as presidential material.

Meanwhile, President Richard Nixon was in deep trouble politically due to the Watergate scandal. Several burglars had broken into offices of the Democratic National Committee in the Watergate building in Washington, D.C. Their intent was to find information that Nixon's supporters could use in the 1972 race for president. Although Nixon claimed he had no part in the break-in, he had worked to cover up the scandal.

Many Republicans deserted Nixon, but Reagan

defended him during the crisis and insisted that the president and his advisers should be considered innocent until proven guilty. Reagan may have believed that, but he had never been a close friend of Nixon, and it was to Reagan's advantage if Nixon finished out his term in office. "Otherwise, Gerald Ford, Nixon's appointed vice president would succeed to the presidency and would almost certainly want to run in 1976," said Bob Schieffer and Gary Paul Gates in a book they wrote about Reagan.[1]

Then it would be difficult for Reagan to oppose Ford, a sitting president; and if Reagan had to wait until 1980 to run for the presidency, voters might view him as too old to hold office.

But eventually, in 1974, Nixon did resign, and Ford replaced him in the White House. Then Ford decided to run for reelection as president. Reagan's supporters still believed, however, that Ford was too closely tied to Nixon's problems. "Hardly a day passed when someone didn't call and ask me to make a run for the Republican presidential nomination," Reagan said.[2]

Trying to pacify Reagan, Ford offered the California governor a cabinet post, but Reagan, some said, had wanted the vice presidency, which Ford gave to Nelson Rockefeller, a Republican whom conservatives like Reagan found too liberal for their taste.

Soon a committee formed to back Reagan's race for the White House. Leading the effort was John Patrick Sears, an ambitious young Washington lawyer who had helped organize the 1968 campaign for Richard Nixon. Reagan took his antigovernment message to the people to test the waters. His speeches repeated the themes he had used in 1964 in support of Barry Goldwater. He railed against big government and high taxes, and he pleaded for vigilance against the menace of communism and the Soviet Union.

In the fall of 1975, Reagan announced his candidacy at the National Press Club, in Washington, D.C. The federal government had become too dependent on a buddy system, he told the press in his announcement speech. Elected officials were too closely tied to the bureaucracy, lobbyists, labor unions, and big business.

After that, Reagan's campaign sputtered. First there was a speech he gave to the Executive Club of Chicago. Titled "Let the People Rule," the speech had been written by staff members who found the old conservative attacks on the federal government stale and unappealing and believed Reagan had to propose new ideas. The speech suggested that government had become too centralized in the hands of federal officials. Programs like welfare, housing, food stamps, and Medicaid should be transferred to the states, the speech said, a move that could cut the federal budget by more than $90 billion.

Reporters and Ford staff members asked embarrassing questions about the proposal, questions that Reagan could not answer because he had read the speech without having given much thought to its ideas. Ford's staff insisted Reagan's plan would cause high unemployment due to federal cutbacks and a slump in construction; some cities and states would go bankrupt if they took over federal pro-

During his second campaign for the Republican presidential nomination, Reagan addresses a Seattle, Washington, crowd in 1976.

REAGAN FOR PRESIDENT

CITIZENS FOR REAGAN COMMITTEE   401 S.W. Stark, Portland,   BOB HAZEN, Chairman

grams; massive tax increases might be needed locally. All Reagan could do was hope that people would forget about the speech as soon as possible.

Still Reagan's private polls gave him a slight edge over Gerald Ford in New Hampshire where the first presidential primary was scheduled for February 1976. But Ford began catching up. Reagan's pollsters wanted him to keep campaigning in New Hampshire up until election day, but somehow his staff never got that message through to Reagan, and he went on to Illinois. When the New Hampshire primary election was held, early returns showed Reagan in the lead. But by morning it was over: Ford had won, 54,824 to Reagan's 53,507.[3]

"Only afterward did friends in New Hampshire tell me that by leaving the state on the eve of the election, I'd sent a message to the voters of New Hampshire that I was taking them for granted," Reagan said.[4]

It was only a small primary, and Reagan had almost defeated a sitting president, but still the press and public saw it as a serious blow to Reagan's candidacy. After that, he lost in Florida and Illinois, too, and Reagan's chances looked very slim. The press kept pressuring him: when would he quit? Reagan told them he would never drop out; he was going all the way to Kansas City, site of the Republican National Convention.

Then several Republican groups asked Reagan to withdraw. Even Barry Goldwater, whom Reagan had once supported when many others deserted him, endorsed Gerald Ford.

Because Reagan looked like a loser, his donations dropped off. The campaign had so many debts that soon it had to pay in advance for advertising, hotel rooms, airplanes, whatever. Even John Sears had begun negotiating behind the scenes with the

Ford camp about the possibility that Reagan would pull out.

The last big test for Reagan was the March 23 primary in North Carolina. If he failed there, it would be over.

Somehow Reagan struck a nerve with voters in that state, particularly by criticizing Ford's foreign policy. He attacked Ford's plan to turn the Panama Canal over to the government of Panama. "We bought it, we paid for it, it's ours and we're going to keep it," he kept saying.[5]

When the votes came in, Reagan had won North Carolina and had kept his campaign on track. Shortly afterward he bought a half hour of time on network television and raised a million and a half dollars. He was back in business.

After that, he won primaries in Alabama, California, Georgia, and Texas. Still he did not have enough delegates to win the nomination, but neither did Ford. Nevertheless, by July the press was saying that Ford had the nomination sewed up because many uncommitted delegates were leaning toward him.

The night of the balloting, Reagan gathered his family for a dinner beforehand to boost their spirits and to tell them he was not going to pull off an upset. When the ballots were taken, Reagan had 1,070 votes, 70 short of the nomination. Ford had 1,187.

Afterward the two met privately, but both men were uncomfortable. Reagan had asked that Ford not offer him the vice presidential nomination, and he did not do so. Instead, Ford picked Senator Robert Dole, a man of whom Reagan approved. Still there were enthusiastic demonstrations and applause for Reagan on the night that Ford and Dole gave their acceptance speeches.

Later Reagan met with the California delegates

and told them he would come back again. He held another meeting with his campaign workers to thank them. In closing, he quoted from an English ballad: "I will lay me down and bleed a while. Though I am wounded, I am not slain. I shall rise and fight again."[6] Ford, of course, went on to lose to Jimmy Carter. Many believed that Ford had been hurt by his ties to Richard Nixon, particularly after he pardoned Nixon.

Would Reagan have won if he had been nominated? Most political experts doubt it. "Most polling data indicates that Reagan still lacked a national following and drew most of his strength from southern and western Republicans," said Michael Schaller, a University of Arizona history professor.[7]

Reagan left Kansas City feeling frustrated but determined to try again. "Ronnie has always believed what his mother taught him—that whatever happens, happens for a purpose," said Nancy Reagan. "As he saw it, he lost the nomination in 1976 because God had other plans for him."[8]

CHAPTER NINE
"THERE YOU GO AGAIN"

After Gerald Ford lost to Jimmy Carter in 1976, Ronald Reagan was ready to try again. He had almost won the nomination; he had almost been able to taste victory. He could not forget it. "After committing ten years of our lives to what we believed in, I just couldn't walk away and say, 'I don't care any more,'" he said.[1]

In a way, time was running out for Reagan. If he won the 1980 election, he would be seventy when he took office—the oldest president in history. If he served two terms, he would be almost eighty when he left the White House. The 1980 elections were his last chance. Already reporters were joking about his age. "I'd never taken naps or dyed my hair, but that hadn't stopped reporters from suggesting that I did," Reagan said.[2]

He had lost some of his hearing, but he still looked young and vigorous. With his good humor and ability to make fun of himself gracefully, Reagan often managed to turn the age issue into an asset. He often told people that when he saw himself in TV reruns of *Knute Rockne, All American,* it was like "seeing a younger son I never knew I had."[3]

A bigger problem for many reporters and voters was the occasional gap that showed up in Reagan's knowledge of current events. Once he could not give a TV interviewer the name of the president of France. Another time, on a visit to Michigan, he couldn't give details about a federal bailout plan for the Chrysler Corporation. Were these slips due to age or just ignorance? Either possibility was alarming, but the public tended to excuse Reagan for such mistakes.

Part of the reason was that events in the White House and the nation were playing into Reagan's hands. Inflation and interest rates soared to new highs; unemployment was on the rise. President Jimmy Carter also had serious problems on the foreign front. Islamic militants had taken over the government of Iran and imprisoned fifty-two American hostages in the U.S. Embassy. Americans viewed the hostage-taking as an insult to our national prestige, and Carter floundered in handling the crisis.

At the same time, a new wave of conservatism was sweeping the nation. Americans wanted to be proud of their country again and were distraught over those who attacked its flag and power. They were also angry at the level of federal spending and the federal deficit, which was approaching the trillion-dollar mark. They were angry at the heavy burden of local taxes, too, and a taxpayers' revolt was brewing. In California in 1978, voters passed Proposition 13, a measure that greatly reduced local taxes; other states followed with similar bills. Reagan had always promoted the idea of tax cuts, and this issue suited his philosophy of government.

The ideas of Barry Goldwater, which had seemed so extreme just a dozen years before, were beginning to appeal to Americans. And they had found a new and more appealing spokesman for the cause— Ronald Reagan.

The new wave conservatives called themselves

the New Right and generally opposed arms control, abortion rights, gay rights, affirmative action employment programs, and the Equal Rights Amendment. Some belonged to fundamentalist and evangelical Christian churches. Although Jimmy Carter was a Baptist and a born-again Christian, most of those among the New Right were more comfortable with Reagan who also claimed to be born-again, although he seldom attended church.

Of course, other Republicans hoped to catch this wave of conservative furor as well and ride it to the White House. Several were poised to enter the presidential race: George Bush, former Texas congressman and head of the Central Intelligence Agency; Senator Robert Dole of Kansas; Senator Howard Baker of Tennessee; Congressmen Philip Crane and John Anderson of Illinois; former Texas governor John Connally.

Although his campaign had begun years before, Reagan officially announced he was running in a November 1979 speech in New York City. Although the first real primary would not be held until February in New Hampshire, an earlier test for the candidates would be a one-day poll of Republican Party members to be held in January in Iowa.

Once again it looked as if Reagan would blunder into a poor start as he had in New Hampshire during the 1976 campaign. For one thing, his campaign staff was headed by John Sears, who had worked for him in 1976 as well and who did not seem to trust Reagan's judgment and ability. "He believed that Reagan needed to be packaged, programmed and kept away from the voters as much as possible," said Edwin Meese, another campaigner who later became Reagan's attorney general.[4]

In addition, Sears was unsure of whether many voters would show up for the Iowa caucuses and whether the outcome actually meant anything. He did believe, however, that Reagan's history in the state as a radio announcer would give him a strong lead. So Reagan campaigned very little in Iowa and did not even show up for a nationally televised debate held in Des Moines. Candidate George Bush claimed that he had spent more days in Iowa than Reagan had spent hours campaigning there.

On election night in Iowa, Reagan was at home in California watching a movie with friends when he heard that Bush had beaten him 33 percent to 30 percent. He was stunned. Had he thrown away yet another nomination? Suddenly he realized he had to go all out for the New Hampshire primary on February 26 and spend more time with voters.

Reagan also faced another difficulty. His campaign staff was in disarray because of friction between his chief organizer, John Sears, and his key assistants, some of whom were people Reagan had worked with in California. The feuding factions fought constantly, and Sears had forced out some key Reagan aides, including Lyn Nofziger and Michael Deaver. Reagan resented these problems, but said little to Sears at first, perhaps because he believed that Sears, a New Yorker, had a better idea of how to win votes on the East Coast than did the Californians who were friends of Reagan's. Still, he found Sears hard to understand. "I look him in the eye, and he looks me in the tie," he said.[5]

Nancy Reagan entered the fray as well. After long days of campaigning in snowy New Hampshire, the Reagans returned to their hotel. While Reagan got ready for bed, unbeknownst to him, Nancy went from room to room to meet with staff members and soothe angry feelings. "When I finally got to bed, Ronnie would ask me where I had been, and I would make up various excuses," she said.[6]

Bush and Reagan were the front-runners in New Hampshire. Friction between the two resulted in a showdown when a New Hampshire newspaper, the *Nashua Telegraph,* offered to hold a debate between them. The other candidates objected that the newspaper was making an illegal campaign contribution to Bush and Reagan by paying for a debate and excluding them. So Reagan suggested to the Bush camp that the two candidates split the cost of the debate. When Bush refused, Reagan's committee decided to fund the entire debate.

Then Reagan decided that as long as he was paying the bill, he would invite the other candidates. Four of them showed up for the event at Nashua High School. That's when the fireworks began.

Bush angrily refused to participate if the other candidates were allowed to speak. Reagan came on stage with the others standing behind him; Bush sat stiffly and silently in his chair. The audience yelled at Bush and demanded that everyone participate. Reagan agreed. At that point the editor of the *Nashua Telegraph* ordered Reagan's microphone turned off. Reagan pounded his fist on the table and yelled. "I paid for this microphone."[7]

In the end, the other candidates left without speaking, and Bush and Reagan held their debate. But what they said counted for little; Reagan had won a dramatic victory with the audience.

A few days later, Reagan won the New Hampshire primary with 51 percent of the vote. George Bush placed a distant third.

On the afternoon of election day, before the votes were counted, Reagan finally fired John Sears and Sears's key workers. Reagan had decided that he favored a more grassroots approach to campaigning than Sears wanted, and Reagan was tired of the friction that Sears caused. He appointed as his new campaign director William J. Casey, who had been the head of the Securities and Exchange Commission. Although Casey did not have much political experience, he had close contacts with company presidents and top financial people—key sources of funds for the Reagan campaign.

From then on, Reagan rolled up primary victories in state after state: Vermont, South Carolina, Alabama, Illinois, Georgia, Florida. Eventually everyone else except for Bush had dropped out of the Republican race. Anderson had decided to become a third party candidate.

When the Republicans held their convention in Detroit in July, there was only one real mystery: who would be the vice presidential nominee? Bush was a leading candidate because he had won the respect of many Republicans during his primary campaign. He was also viewed as more of a moderate than Reagan and thus could balance the ticket.

Some of Reagan's supporters had another idea: why not pick Gerald Ford, who had nearly beaten Jimmy Carter four years before? Reagan and Ford would be a dream ticket, two nearly unbeatable candidates running together. Reagan was interested at first, and so was Ford, but then Reagan got worried about Ford upstaging him. Would Ford, who had once been president, take the backseat to a candidate who had only been a governor? Ford had his doubts too, and eventually withdrew his name.

So as the convention crowd roared its approval, Ronald Reagan announced that his running mate was George Bush.

The nominees, Reagan and Bush, left that convention with a commanding lead in the polls over the incumbent president Jimmy Carter, but soon Reagan and his aides began to make one mistake after another.

With his wife, Nancy, at the Republican National
Convention in Detroit, Michigan, Reagan acknowledges
supporters after winning the Republican presidential
nomination in 1980.

For example, just before appearing before the National Urban League, a black organization in New York, Reagan insisted on making an appearance in Philadelphia, Mississippi, a place where three civil rights workers had been slain in 1964. The awkward combination of the two speeches made him appear to be hardened toward minority groups. He had also referred to Tuscumbia, Alabama, where Jimmy Carter opened his campaign, as the birthplace of the Ku Klux Klan and had to apologize for the remark. He then made some ill-advised comments suggesting that if elected he would reopen relations with the Nationalist Chinese in Taiwan. Unfortunately he made those statements after sending Bush on a friendly mission to the People's Republic of China.

Part of the problem was the lack of experienced political aides around Reagan. Casey was an intelligent man who had reached the top of the financial world, but he was unsure of how to run a political campaign. So Reagan brought in Stuart Spencer, a political consultant who had helped manage his first campaign for governor. Spencer's initial goal was to stop Reagan from speaking to the press without first thinking about what he had to say. "Everything he said had to be scrutinized ten times more than it ever was before," Spencer said.[8]

In other words, Reagan had to keep his mouth shut about topics with which he was unfamiliar. Still, he continued to stumble occasionally, like the time he told an audience of steel and coal company executives that forests were involved in creating air pollution problems.

Members of the press also complained that Reagan sometimes told dramatic, patriotic anecdotes during his speeches that had no basis in fact. One of his favorites was the story of a crew of a U.S.

B-17 bomber that took a direct hit after a bombing mission over Germany. The pilot ordered the crew to bail out, and the men started leaving the plane, except for a young gunner who was wounded and trapped in his seat. The gunner started crying out in terror. As Reagan told the story: "The last man to leave the plane saw the copilot sit down and take the boy's hand and he said, 'Never mind, son, we'll ride it down together.'" The Congressional Medal of Honor was posthumously awarded to the copilot, according to Reagan. But in fact, said Haynes Johnson, a *Washington Post* reporter who covered the campaign, "No such incident is known to have occurred in World War II and no Medal of Honor was awarded for anything resembling this story. The story was either the product of Reagan's imagination or a scene he remembered from a World War II Hollywood movie."[9]

All of this didn't seem to matter to voters, however. They saw Reagan "as a warm, friendly figure who might get a little confused about details from time to time but had no doubt about where he wanted to lead the country."[10]

Reagan's training as an actor helped him a great deal on the campaign trail. He spoke clearly and strongly, he could make fun of himself a little bit, and he made audiences feel relaxed and comfortable.

His performance contrasted strongly with that of President Jimmy Carter, who was under pressure over many issues including the Americans being held hostage in Iran. Instead of hitting Reagan hard on the issues, Carter attacked Reagan in a bitter and personal way that made voters think Carter had a mean streak. Early on, the tense and angry Carter came close to accusing Reagan of being a racist. Later he told a union convention that the elec-

A beaming Ronald Reagan gets the endorsements of two fellow Republicans, former president Gerald Ford (left) and vice-presidential candidate George Bush, on the 1980 presidential campaign trail in Peoria, Illinois.

tion would decide whether the nation had peace or war.

Reagan responded by playing the role of someone unfairly accused and injured. To say that anyone would deliberately seek war is "beneath decency," Reagan replied.[11]

All along, Reagan had favored a debate with Carter. Reagan's staff believed it would be the perfect way for voters to compare the candidates and see that Reagan was not warlike and bigoted, as Carter claimed.

A date was finally set for October 28, a week before the election. Just as Reagan's staff had hoped, the event proved a tremendous success for him. He was strong on defense issues and in his opposition to the Soviet Union, but he also talked about maintaining peace: "I believe with all my heart that our first priority must be world peace and that use of force is always and only a last resort when everything else has failed."[12]

Whenever Carter said something Reagan felt was unfair or unjustified, he responded with "There you go again."[13] That phrase was repeated long afterward by Reagan's supporters and became the one sentence that summed up the debate in many minds.

Carter also made one statement that proved especially embarrassing for him. In discussing arms control, he said that just before the debate he had asked his daughter, Amy, what the most important campaign issue was. "She said she thought nuclear weaponry and the control of nuclear arms."[14]

The remark made Carter look silly. Should a president really ask a twelve-year-old for advice? people wondered.

Throughout the end of the presidential campaign, Reagan held on to a strong lead in the opinion polls, varying from 5 percent to 8 percent. After the debate, he surged ahead. Still his advisers feared that Carter might pull off an "October surprise" if he brought home the hostages from Iran. Then Carter might sweep away many of the doubts that voters had about his leadership.

In fact, just a few days before the election, the Iranian government issued four conditions for release of the Americans. Then Carter announced that the release of the hostages might be close at hand. But the release never came.

Finally the campaign ended and the Reagans returned to California to vote. They planned to eat dinner with friends that night and watch the election returns on television. But while Reagan dressed, he heard on television that the networks had declared him the winner. Soon after that, Carter called to concede. Before the polls closed in California, Reagan knew he was going to the White House.

Not only had Reagan won with an electoral vote count of 489, compared to 49 for Carter, he had also turned Congress upside down. Eleven new Republican senators had been elected, giving the GOP control of the U.S. Senate for the first time in many years.

CHAPTER TEN

"TIME TO REAWAKEN THIS INDUSTRIAL GIANT"

The presidential limousine glided slowly along Pennsylvania Avenue that cloudy and gloomy morning of January 20, 1981. Outgoing President Jimmy Carter and the new president, Ronald Reagan, rode silently to Reagan's inauguration. Carter, his face worn and pale, hardly spoke to or even glanced at the president-elect.

The night before, Carter had slept on a couch in the Oval Office as he waited for word that the American hostages in Iran had been released and flown to Germany. For weeks Carter had hoped that the release would take place before he left office, providing one bright moment in the last dark days of his presidency. But the word never came.

At the Capitol, Reagan took the oath of office with his hand on his mother's Bible, opened to II Chronicles 7:14: "If my people, which are called by my name, shall humble themselves and pray, and seek my face, and turn from their wicked ways; then will I hear from heaven, and will forgive their sin, and will heal their land."

When he went to the podium to give his speech, an unusual thing happened that many reporters commented on. The clouds overhead parted slightly, and the sun shone down on Reagan. "It is time to

President Reagan delivers his inaugural address after taking the oath of office as the nation's fortieth president in front of the Capitol building in Washington, D.C., on January 20, 1981.

reawaken this industrial giant, to get government back within its means, and to lighten our punitive tax burden," he told the crowd.[1]

At lunch Reagan made the announcement that all Americans had been awaiting: Iran had released the fifty-two captives; they were coming home. It was an incredibly lucky event for Reagan. The public seemed to credit him with the responsibility for the release of the hostages even though it was outgoing President Carter who had arranged for their freedom. Americans were relieved and happy. Already it seemed this new president had brought a change of direction for the nation.

Later there were allegations that Reagan's campaign staff might have made a secret deal with Iran to delay the freeing of the hostages until after the inauguration. Three Reagan security advisers later admitted having met with an emissary from Iran in October 1980 and various Iranians later claimed that some kind of deal had been made. But Reagan's staff denied the charges, and no solid proof was ever produced to back up the allegations.

In appointing his cabinet and setting up the new government, Reagan did not simply pick old favorites. Alexander Haig, formerly with President Richard Nixon, was named secretary of state; George Shultz later replaced Haig. James Baker, who had worked for George Bush in the primaries, became Reagan's chief of staff. Edwin Meese and William Casey, who had worked on the Reagan campaign, became attorney general and director of the Central Intelligence Agency. Caspar Weinberger, who had worked for Reagan when he was governor, became the secretary of defense. David Stockman, a former congressman with many strong ideas about taxation and the budget, became the director of the Office of Management and Budget. James Watt became the secretary of the interior. Some of the choices were solid ones; some later involved Reagan in controversy.

Part of the problem was that Reagan declined to involve himself closely in the day-to-day details of what his staff was doing. He expected to provide the core ideas, the inspiration, the leadership challenge for his staff. He expected them to put his policies into action. To a degree, this management style worked better than that of Jimmy Carter, who had gotten buried in the details of everyone's job. But it also meant that many of Reagan's aides could run their offices as they wished with little or no direction from the boss. For example, one group of staff members was assigned to draw up a plan for Reagan's first hundred days in office. They worked very hard on the presentation they were to make to him and tried to come up with the answers to all his possible comments on their ideas. On the big day, they outlined their plan for Reagan and finished by asking if he had any questions. "Sounds great," he said. "Go to it." To their surprise, Reagan did not ask them a single question.[2]

Reagan was preoccupied with "the outer presidency," said Donald T. Regan, who served as Reagan's secretary of the Treasury and later as chief of staff. Reagan didn't call up aides to see if they had followed through on tasks; he didn't discuss the tiniest details of military operations with generals. "In this," Regan said, "he was the antithesis of most recent presidents. . . . He trusted his lieutenants to act on his intentions, rather than on his spoken instructions."[3]

One of his major intentions, of course, was to cut the nation's deficit, the amount of money spent beyond what was received in taxes and fees. To do that, a country can raise taxes, but Reagan had a different approach. His ideas and those of his staff are often referred to as Reaganomics or the Reagan Revolution or supply-side economics. Some of these economic ideas were borrowed from University of Chicago Professor Milton Friedman, who argued that ups and downs in the economy are strongly affected by the size of the money supply set by the Federal Reserve Bank. Friedman also believed in having a free-market economy—that is, one which is free of government regulation—an idea that fit Reagan's political philosophy.

Reagan also favored the view of a University of Southern California professor, economist Albert Laffer, who contended that by slashing tax rates, government could spark an economic boom that would lead to the growth of businesses and higher income for all. The result would be more tax revenue for the government. In other words, the benefits of cutting taxes for businesses and the wealthy would "trickle down" to everyone. Laffer's views had strongly influenced Reagan's director of the Office of Management and Budget, David Stockman.

Cutting tax rates and allowing people to spend or save more of what they earn would make them more industrious, Reagan said. "They'll have more incentive to work hard, and money they earn will add fuel to the great economic machine that energizes our national progress."[4]

Reagan also wanted to cut wasteful government spending, but he did not want to touch the defense budget at all. He believed that years of neglect had drastically weakened the nation's military might compared to that of the Soviet Union. He told the military Joint Chiefs of Staff that he wanted to spend whatever was needed to catch up with the Russians.

The combination of tax cuts and big military

spending was an explosive one. How could he persuade Congress to adopt his ideas? Republicans controlled the Senate, but the House was still in the hands of Democrats. Reagan wanted a 30 percent cut in tax rates over three years as well as lower taxes on capital gains and smaller estate and gift taxes. Meanwhile, he proposed increasing defense spending by three-quarters of a trillion dollars for the next year.

Reagan's director of the budget, David Stockman, aimed to cut the budget by more than $100 billion to offset the tax cuts and defense spending that Reagan was proposing.[5] Although some contended that Reagan was planning an assault on the programs that were set up during Franklin Roosevelt's New Deal in the 1940s, most of the programs that Reagan aimed to cut were the ones established by President Lyndon Johnson as part of his Great Society: child nutrition, subsidies for mass transit, public service jobs. In the end, Reagan ruled out cutting Social Security, Medicare, veterans' benefits, school lunches, Head Start, and summer youth jobs.[6]

The problem was, said Stockman, that Reagan was "too kind, gentle and sentimental."

"Despite his right-wing image, his ideology and philosophy always take a backseat when he learns that some individual human being might be hurt," Stockman said. "That's also why he couldn't lead a real revolution in American economic policy."[7]

Reagan did move, however, toward cutting back on the rules and regulations governing many fields of business and commerce, including air and water purity, banking practices, airlines, nuclear plants, workplace safety, and consumer goods.

Regardless of the questions that were raised about Reagan's proposals, many Americans were interested in seeing Reagan's ideas put to work. They trusted this new president whose relaxed confidence on television made them feel as if they were listening to their grandfather talk to them.

Then an event took place that further sealed Reagan's popularity with the public and, in an unusual way, furthered his policies and power over Congress.

In late March, just sixty-nine days after the inauguration, Reagan went to the Washington, D.C., Hilton Hotel to give a speech. As he left the hotel, he was going to his car when he heard what sounded like firecrackers popping nearby. Suddenly a Secret Service man pushed him into the backseat of the presidential limousine. A sharp pain flashed through Reagan's back; he thought he had broken a rib. He sat up and began to cough up blood until his handkerchief was soaked through. He could hardly breathe. The limousine driver rushed to George Washington University Hospital. Reagan began to walk to the emergency room and then collapsed. Doctors quickly determined that Reagan had been shot and needed surgery. The bullet had struck one of his ribs, glanced off, punctured his lung, and lodged near his heart.

Although Reagan had been seriously injured and was barely conscious, he retained his grace and sense of humor even in these desperate moments. When Nancy Reagan arrived at the hospital, he whispered to her, "Honey, I forgot to duck."[8]

Then as he was entering the operating room, he told the doctors, "Please tell me you're all Republicans." A doctor replied, "We're all Republicans today."[9]

During surgery, doctors repaired damage to the president's lung and removed the bullet. Reagan had survived, although his life was still not out of danger for some time.

Soon after the shooting, officials had captured

the lone gunman involved, John Hinckley, a solitary young man in his mid-twenties who had been obsessed with the idea of killing a president. He had fired six shots from only ten feet away. One had hit James Brady, the White House press secretary; others had hit a Washington policeman and a Secret Service agent.

Confusion struck the White House after the shooting. Reagan had been in office only seventy days; emergency procedures had barely been discussed at that point. In fact, on the day of the shooting, White House staff members had planned to meet with the Secret Service to discuss how to handle an assassination attempt. The meeting was never held.

Vice President George Bush was in Texas for a speech at the time of the attack. At first he was told that Reagan had been shot at but not injured. After finally learning about Reagan's injuries, he returned to Washington.

Meanwhile, at a White House press conference, reporters barraged staff members for information about how badly Reagan was hurt and who was leading the country. Finally, Secretary of State Alexander Haig stepped to the podium. When a reporter asked, "Who is making the decisions for the government right now?" Haig replied: "Constitutionally,

March 30, 1981. Only three months after he took office, Reagan found himself the target of a would-be assassin. Secret Service agents hasten to protect the president as bullets fly.

gentlemen, you have the president, the vice president, the secretary of state in that order. . . . As of now I am in control here in the White House."[10]

Haig was in error; a law passed in 1947 provided that after the vice president, the Speaker of the House, president pro tem of the Senate, and then members of the cabinet would take charge of the U.S. government. Although Haig never really attempted to take charge and probably spoke brashly due to nervousness, his statement aroused criticism in the press and from fellow staff members, particularly from Secretary of Defense Caspar Weinberger.

Even after Bush returned to the White House there was confusion about his role and authority. The law of succession made it possible for Bush to take over the government temporarily during an illness or injury to the president. Instead Bush seemed to take a backseat to other White House insiders. James Baker, Edwin Meese, and Deputy Chief of Staff Michael Deaver seemed to be running the White House in Reagan's absence.[11]

Reagan's staff tried to cover up the extent of Reagan's injuries and how weak and disoriented he was. Perhaps because the administration had just taken over, they feared that the public would think the president could not do his job. Reagan returned to the White House in early April, and in mid-June, only nine weeks after the shooting, he announced that he had fully recovered. His physician, Daniel Ruge, disputed that: "So far as I am concerned, he probably wasn't fully recovered until about October."[12]

But the American public asked few questions. Instead a wave of warmth and acceptance flooded from them to the White House. Once again an assassin had tried to destroy a president, and this time he had failed. Reagan's courage after the shooting and his apparent ability to bounce back despite his age impressed them. His popularity soared. By midsummer, Democrats in Congress had joined Republicans to vote for the tax cuts Reagan wanted and his military spending plan. There was a 5 percent tax cut beginning on October 1, 1981, with 10 percent cuts planned for 1982 and 1983. Military spending was to go up $28 billion in 1981 and even more in 1982.

These bills weren't passed based on Reagan's popularity alone. He worked hard for them and showed a remarkable ability to deal with Democrats in Congress; he was much better at making friends than Carter had been. In about four months in office, Reagan met sixty-nine times with members of Congress—meetings attended by almost five hundred people. Although the southern, more conservative, lawmakers were his closest allies, he also befriended more liberal members of Congress including Speaker of the House Thomas P. O'Neill.

In 1981, Reagan also made a significant appointment to the Supreme Court—Sandra Day O'Connor, an Arizona State Court of Appeals judge. Although O'Connor was a Republican, many New Right leaders opposed her because she was moderate on the abortion issue. Although she had criticized the ruling in *Roe v. Wade,* the 1973 Supreme Court case that secured a woman's right to have an abortion in certain circumstances, and had stated a personal opposition to abortion, she was not against a woman's right to choose. Anti-choice hard-liners wanted a nominee who stood more firmly with them. Reagan would have liked the support of the conservatives in the Senate, but to a degree he welcomed their opposition because he felt it would ensure the support of many conservatives in the liberal Senate who

sought to distance themselves from the far right. When the Senate hearings were completed, O'Connor became the first woman justice in the 191-year history of the high court.

Another tough issue during the 1980s was environmental protection, and from the beginning, Reagan's policies on the environment riled Congress and conservationists. His secretary of the interior, James Watt, was from Wyoming, and, like Reagan, he shared the views of those who were part of the so-called Sagebrush Rebellion—those westerners who thought that the federal agencies had too much to say about use of vast open lands in the West. But Watt's views were even stronger than Reagan's. Watt had been recommended to Reagan by Senator Paul Laxalt of Nevada, a strong supporter of Reagan. Soon after taking office, Watt announced that every year for five years, 200 million acres of offshore land would be opened to oil drilling. Even oil companies were stunned by the plan.

Watt also stopped buying new land for national parks and refused to spend money already set aside for fixing up existing parks. He proposed opening many wilderness areas to oil drilling and hard rock mining. Soon even moderate conservationists and Republican members of Congress were upset and enraged, and Watt had to back down.

Although Reagan did not agree with all of Watt's

In July 1981, Reagan nominated Sandra Day O'Connor, a fifty-one-year-old Arizona Court of Appeals judge, to the U.S. Supreme Court. Her confirmation marked the first time a woman filled a seat on the nation's highest court.

proposals, he allowed the secretary a free hand and stepped in only when the public outcry became very strong. Eventually, in October 1983, Watt was forced to resign after he made a racially insensitive remark during a speech to the U.S. Chamber of Commerce. Toward the end of the summer of 1981, Reagan was caught in a struggle with a powerful union, a conflict that ended up increasing his popularity and reputation. On August 3, the Professional Air Traffic Controllers Organization voted to strike. The 11,600 controllers, who directed traffic at the nation's airports, were upset about their heavy workload and the delays and traffic jams on the runways. But the strike was an illegal one; there was a no-strike clause in their contract.

Reagan quickly set a deadline for the controllers to be back on the job; when they failed to meet the deadline, he fired them all and ordered military controllers to staff commercial airport towers. New controllers were eventually hired to replace the fired strikers.

The situation could have been negotiated in a more moderate way. But the public had grown tired of union tactics, and they approved of Reagan's quick, firm response to the crisis, however heavy-handed it might have been.

In this situation, and many times during his presidency, even when the president made mistakes in his speeches or blundered in some way, blame never seemed to stick to him. The press often referred to him as the "Teflon president" because of this. Fellow politicians and reporters were puzzled by the phenomenon. Was it due to the incredible luck he had had all of his life? Did people excuse him for his mistakes because of his folksy personality? Was it simply because he was the most beloved president in decades?

Or perhaps it was because the press simply didn't go after Reagan as fiercely as they had gone after presidents in the past. One of Reagan's aides, David Gergen, suggested: "I think a lot of the Teflon came because the press was holding back. I don't think they wanted to go after him that toughly."[13]

Many in the press seemed to think, according to Gergen, that after Watergate and Vietnam, the public was tired of seeing the press attack the president. Maybe it was time to give the nation's president a little more leeway.

At any rate, by the middle of Reagan's first term, the economy had improved. Interest rates dropped, the cost of imported gas and oil came down. Heavier military spending created new jobs in the computer and aerospace industries.

Reagan and his staff believed that their tax cuts and the move to deregulate business and industry were sparking the economic boom. Others had their doubts; they believed that the country was borrowing against its future. While military spending grew enormously, other government expenditures were not being cut back as much as Reagan had hoped. Even Reagan's budget director, David Stockman, was growing skeptical. "After November 1981, the administration locked the door on its own disastrous fiscal policy jail cell and threw away the key," Stockman said. "The president would not let go of his tax cut. Cap Weinberger hung on for dear life to the $1.46 trillion defense budget. . . . The nation's huge fiscal imbalance was never addressed or corrected; it just festered and grew."[14]

In an article written about him in the *Atlantic Monthly,* Stockman expressed his fears that the deficit would balloon dangerously. The article embarrassed both Reagan and Stockman. Could the budget director really be abandoning the principles of the Reagan Revolution? the press wanted to know. Reagan believed, however, that Stockman had been sabotaged by the press and declined to ask him to resign. After that, Stockman kept his mouth shut and did what he could to reduce the deficit. But his predictions came to pass: over the next eight years the national debt nearly tripled to almost $2.7 trillion. Reagan blamed Congress for much of this debt. Tax revenues increased despite his tax cuts, but Congress kept spending, he argued. "If I'd gotten cuts I proposed in 1981, for example, the cumulative deficit between 1982 and 1986 would have been $207 billion less than it was."[15]

Other major changes were taking place in the economy as well. By the mid-1980s, the country had been swept by a new furor of corporate mergers and takeovers, made possible by easier credit policies in banks and savings and loan associations. Companies were going into heavy debt to swallow up other companies. Some takeovers were financed by means of junk bonds—that is, high-interest, high-risk bonds sold to raise money to buy companies. These bonds were risky because in many cases the bond holders could not be paid off from the cash flow of the purchased companies.

In financing these takeovers and other questionable business and real estate deals, banks and savings and loans seriously impaired their financial stability.

Because of a deregulation act endorsed by Reagan and passed in 1982, it had become much easier to open new savings and loan associations. In many cases the new S&L entrepreneurs used their businesses to finance luxurious lifestyles. Deregulation also allowed savings and loans to turn from financing home mortgages—their primary business in the past—to financing risky business ventures,

including junk bond deals. Reagan was not person-
ally responsible for all this, but in a report issued
near the end of his administration, even White
House economists blamed the savings and loan crisis on the federal deregulation that Reagan had
favored.

Eventually, by 1991, more than six hundred savings and loans had failed, and the government had
to set up a special corporation to manage the land
and buildings owned by these defunct organizations.
Clearly, taxpayers would have to pay billions to pay
off the debts of these failed savings and loans.

Meanwhile the United States was piling up debt
with other countries. In 1980 the value of foreign
imports exceeded the value of what the United
States exported by $26 billion. By the end of the
1980s the country had a trade deficit of more than
$150 billion a year.

But the troubles that would arise out of all this
financial confusion seemed far away at the time. In
the early 1980s, Americans believed that the economy was picking up. Life seemed to be getting better, and the man responsible for that seemed to be
Ronald Reagan.

CHAPTER ELEVEN
FOREIGN AFFAIRS

The country of Lebanon lies on a narrow strip of land on the Mediterranean Sea, where it is hemmed in by Syria to the east and north and Israel to the south. Since 1975 this Middle Eastern nation had been torn by civil war between Christians and Muslims, who had also split into splinter groups that feuded with each other as well. For Ronald Reagan, Lebanon became a firestorm that threatened to cancel out his accomplishments as president and turn his popularity with the American people to ashes.

In Reagan's first year in office, his main concern had been what he could do domestically for the United States—cutting taxes and federal spending, removing government regulations.

But soon the outside world intruded—in particular, the Middle East. In Libya, a flamboyant dictator, Muammar al-Qaddafi, had taken over the country and beefed up his military forces using arms and planes purchased from the Soviet Union. Qaddafi also appeared to be funding terrorist groups in the Middle East and Europe. Anxious to put Qaddafi in his place, the United States sent ships and aircraft on maneuvers in the Gulf of Sidra on the Libyan coast. When Libyan jets began harassing American ships, Reagan authorized U.S. Navy pilots to pursue them. The next time it happened, American F-14s shot down two Libyan aircraft.

Qaddafi had been set back for a time, but new problems had developed in Lebanon. In July 1981, Syria and Israel were about to go to war using Lebanon as their battleground. Israel wanted to wipe out the camps of the Palestinian Liberation Organization in Lebanon. Syria, like other Muslim nations in the Middle East, was bent on destroying Israel.

Reagan sent a peace envoy, Philip Habib, who arranged a cease-fire that lasted about a year. But in June 1982, Israel launched a massive invasion of Lebanon and pounded west Beirut for days with bombs. Thousands of uninvolved civilians were killed or injured.

The bloody violence shocked Reagan, who had always supported Israel. When Israeli Prime Minister Menachem Begin visited Reagan in late June, the president insisted that Israel stop the war and begin talks with the Palestinians. But the sickening attacks on homes and families in Beirut continued.

On August 12, 1982, Israeli planes bombed west Beirut for eleven hours straight. At that point a Reagan staff member told the president he wanted to resign. "I can't be a part of this any more, the bombings, the killing of children," he said. "You're the one person on the face of the earth right now who can stop it. All you have to do is tell Begin you want it stopped."[1]

Reagan, too, was horrified. He called Begin and told him that Israel was creating a "holocaust" in Beirut. The symbol of Israel was becoming "a picture of a seven-month-old baby with its arms blown off," he said.[2]

Reagan's firm stand had an effect; soon afterward, the bombing stopped. Meanwhile, Reagan's envoy, Habib, arranged a cease-fire under which the warring armies would pull out and let the Lebanese government take control. A key part of the agreement called for setting up a multinational peacekeeping force. Supposedly many nations would join this effort, but the United States supplied most of the soldiers. Overseeing the withdrawal of tens of thousands of Israeli and Syrian troops were a mere 800 U.S. Marines and 350 French paratroopers.

Many of Reagan's advisers opposed sending in these marines and getting so directly involved in the Middle Eastern turmoil. At first all went smoothly, however. The Israelis and Syrians pulled out, and the marines returned to their ships in the Mediterranean.

Then, in mid-September, the new president of Lebanon, a Christian leader named Bashir Gemayel, was assassinated in a bombing. The Israelis used this as justification for marching back into west Beirut, and the Lebanese militia swept through Palestinian refugee camps run by the Israelis and massacred seven hundred people, many of them women and children. The Israelis did nothing to stop the slaughter.

The horrifying nightmare led Reagan to return the marines to Lebanon. For a while the violence slowed down, but it did not stop. In April 1983 the U.S. Embassy was bombed and sixty-three people were killed, including many Central Intelligence Agency representatives who were providing the State Department with vital information about the conflict.

All through this, Reagan's staff had been in turmoil on the issue of Lebanon, and the confusion grew worse when Secretary of State Alexander Haig resigned. Haig had been having frequent turf battles with other staff members and had also irritated Reagan with his demands. Reagan appointed George Shultz, president of the Bechtel Corporation, to replace Haig.

Neither Haig nor Shultz had a clear idea of how to handle the problems in Lebanon. Each time disas-

Marines carry the body of one of their own from the
rubble in the aftermath of the October 1983 terrorist
bombing of a U.S. Marine barracks in Beirut, Lebanon.
The 1980s saw a significant increase in the use of
terrorism against the United States.

ter struck, the cabinet wrangled about who was to blame and who should do what. At times, some observers said, it seemed that Reagan was more involved in keeping peace among his cabinet members than in taking decisive action in Lebanon.

When the marines first returned to Lebanon, they were viewed by the Muslim groups as saviors who would stop the bloodshed. By the fall of 1983, however, they were seen as the enemy, particularly after U.S. ships fired on Muslim armed groups on shore in order to protect the Lebanese army. The Israelis had pulled their troops out, and the marines seemed to be the only force backing up the minority Christian government of Lebanon.

Dispute raged in Washington over what the marines should do. Reagan had a new security adviser, Robert "Bud" McFarlane, who wanted them to stay in Lebanon. The Joint Chiefs of Staff, leaders of the nation's military forces, wanted them to pull out, as did Secretary of Defense Caspar Weinberger. Weinberger believed that the marines were easy targets for Muslim terrorists. But the fact that the nation's top military leaders wanted to withdraw the marines was not made public.

Early on a Sunday morning, October 23, 1983, disaster struck. A lone terrorist drove a truck into the barracks building in Beirut where 350 members of the First Battalion Eighth Marine Regiment were sleeping. The truck, loaded with 12,000 pounds of TNT, exploded, and the building collapsed. In all, 241 marines died; another 112 were injured, many of them seriously.

Two miles away in west Beirut, a bomb destroyed another building and killed fifty-eight French paratroopers who, like the marines, had come to Lebanon to keep the peace. Angry Americans recoiled in horror. Were they about to embark on a new Vietnam War that would kill thousands of young men? How could conventional military forces deal with terrorists on suicide missions like the one that slaughtered the marines? Reagan wanted to retaliate, but there was little American forces could do that would not end up killing or injuring civilians. Eventually the remaining marines were pulled out.

Simultaneously another crisis was brewing on the Caribbean island of Grenada, where the prime minister had been deposed and killed. The military group that took over was closely allied with Fidel Castro, dictator of Cuba. Cuban laborers were being used to build an airport runway that U.S. officials believed would be used to fly supplies to Marxists throughout Central America. Reagan's advisers had told him that they also believed that eight hundred American medical students at Saint George's University in Grenada were in danger because of the military coup.

Just one day after the tragedy in Beirut, Reagan agreed to send American forces to attack Grenada. That operation was a huge success. Some five thousand American troops invaded Grenada and restored order. The Cubans were returned to their country, and massive numbers of weapons were found. Only nineteen Americans died in the invasion, and the medical students were rescued. The easy victory in Grenada seemed to wash away the dishonor and shame Americans had felt about Lebanon.

Some suspected that the Reagan administration might have been trying to cover up the events in Lebanon with the Grenada invasion. In fact, the planning for Grenada had been going on for several days before the attack in Lebanon; at one point, Reagan had considered scrapping the invasion due to the death of the marines.

But once the invasion of Grenada was proclaimed a success, Reagan and his staff seemed eager to use the victory to their advantage. In a television speech a few days later Reagan told Americans: "The events in Lebanon and Grenada, though oceans apart, are closely related. Not only has Moscow assisted and encouraged violence in both countries, but it provides direct support through a network of surrogates and terrorists."[3]

Grenada had partly made up for Lebanon in Reagan's mind; the polls showed that Americans agreed with him. In part that may have been because the Reagan administration kept the press from covering the Grenada invasion. It might have seemed like overkill for a giant nation to invade a tiny island in this way, but Americans never got to see pictures of the dead Grenadian troops or of the ruined homes and property. The press was not notified in advance about the invasion, and no reporters were allowed to go with the troops. Later Reagan's staff released "its own sanitized videotapes of the operation," which the three major television networks ran. "Their pictures weren't lying, but because they weren't all the pictures, they ended up being distorting," said John McWethy, an ABC correspondent.[4]

The administration would have a harder time controlling events in Lebanon. Eventually the turmoil of the Middle East would shake the Reagan presidency to its core.

President and Mrs. Reagan attend a memorial service in November 1983 for the people killed in the Marine barracks bombing in Beirut and the U.S. attack on Grenada.

CHAPTER TWELVE
MORNING AGAIN IN AMERICA

As warm family scenes and a waving American flag flashed across the TV screen, a narrator's smooth voice told the viewers: "It's morning again in America. Today, more men and women will go to work than ever before in our country's history."

Interest rates had dropped dramatically, the announcer went on, inflation had also dropped; Americans could look toward the future with confidence. "Under the leadership of President Reagan, our country is stronger and prouder and better. Why would we ever want to return to where we were less than four short years ago?"[1]

These political ads, designed to make Americans feel good about their country, were the main theme of Ronald Reagan's reelection campaign in 1984. As the commercials said, Americans were feeling better about the economy. They had gone through a tragedy in Lebanon, but they could see that their military was still strong and powerful through the events that had occurred in Grenada.

Even reporters seemed to believe that Reagan had put the nation back on the right track again, despite his shortcomings. "The press covering Reagan got caught up in the very mood that the Reagan people wanted them to get caught up in, the theme of their campaign, which was essentially: keep the country dumb, numb and happy," said Robert Beckel, a campaign official for Walter Mondale, the Democratic challenger in the presidential race.[2] Faced with all this patriotic euphoria, Mondale had a tough road ahead of him. Mondale had chosen Geraldine Ferraro, a congresswoman from New York, as his running mate and vice presidential nominee. It was a choice designed to attract women voters, but even this bold move seemed to have little impact on the race.

There had been some question at first about whether Reagan would seek a second term. His wife, Nancy, one of his strongest political advisers, had urged him not to run. She missed California, and she worried about the possibility of another assassin attacking him. She had also taken a beating in the press about her remodeling of the White House, a project funded by millionaire Republican donors, and the fabulous clothes that famous designers loaned to her. She was upset about the intense media attention focused on problems that the Reagans had with their children, particularly Patti, who often disagreed with her father's political views. In the end, Nancy agreed her husband had to try again. "For a while, we talked about it every night, until it became more and more obvious that this was something Ronnie just had to do," she said.[3]

Reagan believed he still had much to accomplish—in particular, balancing the federal budget, a task he had come nowhere near completing in his first four years.

As Reagan's staff saw it, the biggest problem during the presidential race was preventing Reagan from making some kind of super bumble or error. Such a mistake might make voters think that Reagan, at seventy-three, was no longer able to handle the presidency.

So Reagan was shielded from much contact with reporters, and his personal appearances were limited. The strategy worked well early in the campaign; polls showed that at times Reagan had almost a 20 percentage point lead over Mondale. In early October the first of the presidential debates was held in Louisville, Kentucky. Mondale had prepared carefully for the event. He had lots of practice, having debated his Democratic challengers in the primary campaign. His strategy was to attack Reagan aggressively on the issues to try to make it seem that Reagan was no longer quite up to the job. One of Mondale's political advisers told him that the public probably did not even realize that Reagan was having more trouble hearing and following arguments than he had a few years before.

Meanwhile, Reagan had gone through some practice debates with staff, but the truth was that his debating skills had grown rusty. His aides had isolated him so much from contact with the press and public that his speaking skills had deteriorated. He was also not as familiar with the issues as he should have been. A briefing book was prepared for him, but he hardly touched it until just before the debate. At that point he apparently tried to cram facts into his head.

On debate night the well-prepared Mondale looked sharp and skillful, whereas Reagan seemed inept. "Right from the start, he was tense, muddled, and off-stride. He lacked authority. He stumbled," Nancy Reagan said.[4] "What have you done to my husband?" she demanded angrily of staff members.[5] After the debate, Reagan insisted he had stuffed too many facts and figures into his head and spent too much time preparing. "On the night of the debate, I think I was just overtrained," he said.[6]

For the first time the press zeroed in on the question of Reagan's competency to serve as president. For some time reporters had seen Reagan bumble in his statements about the issues and had held back from criticizing him in their stories. But now his faltering performance gave them an opening to inform the public about the president. The very next day a headline in the *Wall Street Journal* read: "Oldest President Now Showing His Age?"[7] Other reporters soon followed with similar stories. The man who had once been called "the great communicator" by the press seemed unable to get his campaign message across.

Reagan was deeply disturbed, and so was Nancy. She angrily confronted his staff. Obviously they were to blame for this debacle. She hadn't wanted her husband to run for president again and now the whole campaign might end in his humiliation.

A second debate was scheduled to take place in another two weeks. Polls showed that Mondale's popularity was growing, although still he was nowhere near catching the president. But another bad performance in the second debate could prove crucial in the campaign and swing many voters to Mondale.

Reagan's staff focused on restoring his confidence as well as coaching him on the facts. Knowledge of statistics was not so important to Reagan, his staff decided, as was the need for him to feel comfortable during the debate.

The second debate, held in Kansas City, focused on foreign affairs, a subject about which Reagan knew a great deal. He not only handled the facts fairly well but also came up with a smashing answer to the question that had troubled Americans since Louisville. One reporter who served on a panel for the debate noted that Reagan was the oldest president in history and asked if he was worried about

Reagan celebrates his reelection to a second term
as president in Los Angeles on November 6, 1984.
Ever popular with the American people, Reagan won reelection easily even though his administration was plagued by
allegations of wrongdoing.

whether he could still handle the pressures of the most important job in the world.

"Not at all," Reagan said with a straight face. "And I want you to know that I will not make age an issue of this campaign. I am not going to exploit, for political purposes, my opponent's youth and inexperience."[8]

The crowd broke into laughter; even Mondale had to chuckle. Reagan had done it again. He had erased the worries of Americans with his good humor. Clearly he seemed ready and able to handle the presidency; his ability to think on his feet was still sharp.

Perhaps Reagan would have won the election anyway, but the successful debate in Kansas City assured him of victory. He won forty-nine states, while Mondale carried only his home state of Minnesota and the District of Columbia. Reagan had 59 percent of the popular vote.

The people of America had given Reagan a mandate to continue the work begun in his first term. They wanted the economic good times of the 1980s to keep on rolling along; they believed Reagan could accomplish that. For Reagan, however, the next four years would begin a slide into turmoil that would end in near-disaster for his presidency.

CHAPTER THIRTEEN
COVERT OPERATIONS

It was supposed to be a glorious trip, one that would show that Reagan was a master of foreign policy. At the beginning of his second term, he planned to attend an economic summit in Bonn, West Germany. There he would have discussions with the top leaders of Europe, including a special friend, Margaret Thatcher, prime minister of England. Reagan had first met her in 1975, before he became president, and soon after that she had become the Conservative Party leader. The two had similar views on economics and remained close even though they sometimes clashed over U.S. foreign policy.

After the summit, Reagan would pay a solemn visit to Bitburg, a German military cemetery, and make a speech honoring the dead of World War II. The idea was that Reagan would be helping to heal wounds from that war while reinforcing the friendship that had united West Germany and the United States for forty years.

Instead the event blew up into a political fiasco. The problem was that among more than two thousand soldiers buried at Bitburg were forty-eight SS storm troopers, soldiers responsible for some of the worst crimes committed by Nazi Germany during World War II, including the murder of Jews and innocent civilians. Reagan and his staff had not known this when the visit was booked, nor had they investigated the cemetery thoroughly enough.

Veterans, Jewish groups, and dozens of senators demanded that Reagan drop the cemetery visit from his trip; even Nancy Reagan urged him not to go. Reagan was deeply offended by charges that he might be anti-Semitic. Nothing had shocked him more after World War II, he said, than the films made by the U.S. Army of prisoners released from the Nazi death camps. Still he kept insisting he had to visit Bitburg; he would embarrass West German Chancellor Helmut Kohl if he canceled, he said.

Finally a compromise was made. Reagan would visit the site of the former Bergen-Belsen concentration camp as well as the cemetery. There he gave a moving speech before mass graves filled with the bodies of thousands of Jews and others slaughtered by the Nazis. After that, he went on to Bitburg.

Those who had protested his German visit were somewhat appeased, but not completely. The embarrassing incident served as an omen of trouble ahead in Reagan's second term. Some of that trouble would come as a result of staff changes.

Reagan, of course, had always depended heavily on his smart and talented aides and cabinet members. When his second term began, many key people decided to leave their jobs, creating turmoil inside the White House. Perhaps these departing staff members could not have saved him from the mistakes of his second term as several of them blundered seriously after leaving the White House. Assistant Chief of Staff Michael Deaver opened a public relations firm and was convicted of lying to Congress about his attempts to use his government connections to improve his business. White House aide Lyn Nofziger also became a lobbyist and was convicted of violating the Ethics in Government Act, although the conviction was later overturned. These scandals reflected poorly on Reagan's judgment in picking staff members.

Early in the second administration Reagan also nominated presidential counselor Edwin Meese to become attorney general. The Senate eventually confirmed the appointment although Meese was plagued by claims that he filed false tax returns and had received payoffs from parties seeking government favors. Many wondered how Meese could head the Justice Department when he lacked good judgment about ethics in government.

Some of the departing staff members felt that the president and Nancy Reagan did not appreciate them. Some were tired of dealing with Nancy's whims and foibles. She had been a strong counselor to the president at times, but after he was shot in the assassination attempt, she had become increasingly dependent on astrology. Often she threw Reagan's schedule into an uproar with her demands that his official appearances be scheduled according to the position of the stars and planets. Keeping her happy required much special attention from the staff.

Early in Reagan's second term, his chief of staff, James Baker, decided he had had enough of all this. He and the secretary of the Treasury, Donald Regan, worked out a plan to switch jobs. Reagan agreed, perhaps not realizing fully how much Baker had done for him. Baker was well liked in Congress and had made many political friends. Although there had been conflicts in the White House while Baker was there, the arguments often helped make Reagan more aware of important problems and questions. "The first failure of Reagan's second term was that he made no effort whatsoever to keep intact the team that had worked so well for him," said Lou Cannon, a reporter who covered Reagan for the *Washington Post*.[1]

On the surface, the job switch did not seem like such a bad idea. Regan was highly intelligent and had served as president of Merrill Lynch, the huge Wall Street brokerage firm. As secretary of the Treasury, he had spent most of 1984 working on a plan for income tax reform. That tax reform act was one of the main goals that Reagan had set for his second term.

"The existing tax system was widely perceived to be incomprehensible in its details and shady in its exceptions," Donald Regan said, "and its replacement by a fair and rational structure that placed all taxpayers on the same footing would certainly be regarded by all people . . . as a great act of presidential leadership," Donald Regan said.[2]

Although the Tax Reform Act passed in 1986 probably fell short of Regan's goals, it did remove many tax shelters and loopholes that benefited wealthier taxpayers. Deductions for business entertainment and travel were curtailed. Deductions for first and second homes were retained, but interest on car loans, credit cards, and life insurance policies became nondeductible. Before, there had been many tax brackets, but now there were just three: 15 percent, 28 percent, and 33 percent. That meant, for example, that a taxpayer paid 15 percent of his taxable income to the government if he was in the lowest bracket. The brackets are based on salary and other income, minus deductions and credits. Some of the poorest Americans no longer had to pay taxes; but some of the richest actually dropped into a lower bracket.

Donald Regan had worked hard on this tax reform plan and helped the president make it a reality.

But inside the White House in his new job as chief of staff, Donald Regan was not as good at handling the sensitive egos of politicians as Baker had been. He was not as skillful at dealing with Nancy Reagan, either. The aides he chose proved more loyal to him than to the president. This new upheaval in the White House soon helped lead to the biggest crisis in Reagan's presidency—the Iran-Contra affair.

The circumstances surrounding the Iran-Contra affair are complicated and cover events of several years. In 1985 and 1986, Reagan and his administration secretly arranged for the sale of antitank and antiaircraft weapons to the Middle Eastern nation of Iran to use in its war against Iraq. These actions violated a U.S. embargo on arms sales to Iran, which had been a foe of the United States ever since the hostage crisis that took place during Jimmy Carter's administration. In return for the weapons, Iran was supposed to arrange for the release of a number of American hostages being held by Muslim groups in war-torn Lebanon. This process violated Reagan's sworn policy that he would never negotiate with terrorists or trade anything to them in return for hostages. Creating even greater difficulties for Reagan, some of the profits from the arms sales were then forwarded to the Contras, rebel soldiers in Central America who were fighting the Nicaraguan government, which was controlled by the Sandinista Party.

To understand the Iran-Contra affair, it's necessary to go back to the beginning of Reagan's first term. Reagan, the staunch anti-Communist, viewed the Contras as freedom fighters, something like the American colonists who had fought their British rulers for freedom. The Sandinistas were Marxists who received aid from Soviet Russia and had refused to hold free elections. But the Sandinistas had also

Marine lieutenant colonel Oliver North is sworn in
before the congressional committee investigating the
Iran-Contra affair, a scandalous episode in American
politics that exposed an administration run amok
under the nose of a distracted president.

overthrown a brutal dictator, Anastasio Somoza in 1979, and some of the Contras were former supporters of Somoza. Reagan believed, however, that if the Sandinistas were not stopped, communism might spread across all Central America. "What is going on is a general revolution aimed at all of Central America, and yes, Mexico," Reagan wrote in his diary early in his first administration.[3]

Early in Reagan's first term he signed orders authorizing the Central Intelligence Agency to arm, feed, and supervise the Contras. Congress at first supported these efforts. But gradually public opinion turned against the Contras. Many members of Congress feared that the Contras could entangle the United States in a war just like that in Vietnam. So in 1983, Congress banned any Contra aid for the purpose of overthrowing the Sandinistas; then, in 1984, Congress put a limit of $24 million on aid to the Contras.

A new crisis arose in 1984 when it was disclosed that the CIA, in support of the Contras, had helped mine the harbors in Nicaragua without notifying Congress. In retaliation furious members of Congress passed the Boland Amendment to cut off all funds for military support of the Contras. The amendment banned any government agency from supporting "directly or indirectly" any military operations in Nicaragua. It also said that such support could be renewed only if the president came back to Congress and persuaded members to change their minds.

The message was clear, but still William Casey, director of the Central Intelligence Agency, pushed Reagan and his key advisers to approve a secret plan to find money to keep the Contras going. Since the CIA had been barred from taking an active role in organizing the Contras, the president's national security adviser, Robert McFarlane, appointed U.S. Marine Lieutenant Colonel Oliver North, a member of Reagan's National Security Council staff, to take over that role. North was also assigned to raise funds from wealthy private citizens and foreign governments, such as Saudi Arabia, in order to keep the Contras going. In 1984 and 1985 some $34 million was secretly raised from other countries and $2.7 million was provided by private contributors. North also enlisted a retired air force general, Richard Secord, and an Iranian-American arms dealer, Albert Hakim, to buy arms secretly for the Contras.

The president and his staff repeatedly denied that these activities were taking place or insisted that no laws were broken. At one point in 1985, when newspapers reported that funds were being raised for the Contras, Reagan assured the public in no uncertain terms that the law was being followed.

Reagan later apologized for what went on and said that as president he bore full responsibility for the situation. But he also contended that much of it happened without his knowledge. This seems very difficult to believe because McFarlane insisted the president had urged him to find some way to keep the Contras going. Furthermore, early in 1985, Saudi Arabia's King Fahd had even informed Reagan about how much money he was providing for the Contras' cause, and Reagan had thanked him.

Congressional investigators later reported as well that Reagan had heard the plan discussed at a meeting in 1984 where staff members had argued over whether the secret aid was legal or not. Secretary of State George Shultz had told Reagan then that if the U.S. government was involved in funneling aid from other countries to the Contras it could be an "impeachable offense."[4]

But Reagan refused to admit that he understood

the situation. McFarlane, Casey, and others knew how worried he was about the Contras, he said later, and that might have led them to embark on the aid plan without his direct approval.

But even if he was deceived about what was going on, why didn't he read the signs or ask more questions?

"Central America was only one of many things that occupied me at the time," Reagan said.[5] He claimed he was also occupied with the recession and cutting government spending, the tax reform act, and the war in Lebanon. If that was the case, his passive attitude toward his staff's actions had reached the point of negligence.

Things almost get out of hand as Reagan and British prime minister Margaret Thatcher attempt to control the Reagan pet, Lucky, in the White House Rose Garden. Agreeing on most economic and foreign policy matters, Reagan and Thatcher quickly developed a mutual respect and close friendship.

CHAPTER FOURTEEN
NEGOTIATING WITH TERRORISTS

On June 14, 1985, one month after Reagan came back from Germany, a TWA plane bound for Rome was hijacked by two Arabs who forced the pilot to fly to Beirut. There were 153 passengers and crew members aboard, including 135 Americans. One of the Americans, a U.S. Navy diver, was shot and killed. Eventually the hostages from the plane were released after negotiations conducted with the help of Syria and Iran. As part of the agreement with the hijackers, Israel, urged on by Reagan, promised to free 700 Shiite Muslims captured during the war in Lebanon.

The process violated many rules that Reagan himself had set for handling terrorists. The United States would not negotiate for hostages, he had insisted. It would not make trades for them. Terrorists would be punished, he had promised, even though it was almost impossible to fulfill that pledge.

Meanwhile, of course, Muslim groups in Lebanon had been taking hostages from the United States and other countries all during 1984 and 1985. By midsummer 1985 seven Americans were in Muslim hands. As the weeks and months passed, Reagan grew more frustrated about this. He was president of the most powerful country in the world, yet he could not protect U.S. citizens against the actions of small groups of guerrillas and terrorists. Meanwhile the families of hostages were pressuring the president. If Reagan would negotiate in the case of the plane hijacking, they said, why wouldn't he negotiate for the lives of their loved ones?

According to Donald Regan, Reagan's chief of staff, the president, because of his background in acting, could easily put himself into the place of the hostages and imagine their agony. As Regan put it about his boss: "All of a sudden he's envisioning himself as a captive alone in a dank, damp prison, and where's the president of the United States?"[1]

When he welcomed home the freed TWA passengers, Reagan told them that the nation would not forget the navy man who had been killed: "His murderers must be brought to justice. Nor will we forget the seven Americans who were taken captive before you."[2]

In July 1985, Israeli officials came to Robert McFarlane, Reagan's national security adviser, with a new idea. According to the Israelis, there were some moderate officials inside the Iranian government who wanted to rebuild their nation's friendship with the United States. The right-wing ruler of Iran, the Ayatollah Khomeini, was growing old; he might die soon. When he did, the moderates might take over and smooth differences with the West. Furthermore, the Israelis believed that these moderates could arrange to free some American hostages being held in Lebanon. There was just one catch: as a token of good faith, Israel would have to sell some high-technology weapons to Iran for use in its war against Iraq. Israel would not do this without U.S. approval.

The contact between these supposed Iranian moderates and Israel and the United States was

Manucher Ghorbanifar, an Iranian merchant living in exile in Paris. In the past, Ghorbanifar had tried to sell information about Iran to the Central Intelligence Agency. The CIA had found him untrustworthy and labeled him a nuisance and a liar. Despite Ghorbanifar's bad reputation, McFarlane was interested. To McFarlane, the plan resembled the secret negotiations that President Richard Nixon had embarked on in the 1970s to open up Red China to the West. McFarlane also knew how important the hostage issue had become to President Reagan.

In mid-July, McFarlane presented the plan to the president, but exactly what McFarlane said and how Reagan reacted is in dispute. At the time, Reagan was in the hospital undergoing surgery for cancer of the colon. As a result, he could have been under physical and emotional stress that impaired his judgment in some way. In addition, McFarlane was not an effective speaker who could explain his ideas clearly. Reagan's chief of staff, Donald Regan, was present, but very few notes were taken. According to Regan, "There is nothing in my notes or in my memory to suggest that the idea of swapping arms for hostages was mentioned by either man on this occasion."[3]

But certainly Reagan understood at the time that McFarlane wanted to negotiate with the Iranians and that McFarlane might get some of the hostages back. Reagan also agreed that the plan might lead to friendship between the United States and Iran once the ayatollah died. "I wanted to explore any avenue that offered the possibility of getting the hostages out of Lebanon," Reagan said later in his autobiography.[4]

At some point, however, McFarlane made clear to Reagan that to get the hostages back, the Israelis had to sell some TOW (tube-launched, optically tracked, wire-guided) antitank missiles to Iran. Israel was willing to do so; it had a surplus of these weapons, which many military experts considered outmoded anyway. Reagan claimed that at first he said no, the United States could not do business with countries that sponsored terrorists, as Iran did. But later he agreed to go ahead. "I was told that Israeli Prime Minister Shimon Peres was behind the proposal and that the Israelis involved in the secret contacts with Iran were all close to Peres," he said.[5]

In early August, McFarlane even talked to the president about all this at a meeting attended by Vice President George Bush, Defense Secretary Caspar Weinberger, Chief of Staff Donald Regan, and Secretary of State George Shultz. Weinberger and Shultz, who often clashed with each other, agreed this time: the plan was wrong and unethical.

Both men advised the president that the proposal simply amounted to an arms-for-hostages trade, regardless of what the Israelis said. After all, the Israelis wanted the United States to sell them more missiles in return for whatever weapons they supplied to Iran. But Reagan, still very concerned about the hostages, wanted to press on. He did warn McFarlane to "go slow"[6] and said he made no decision at the meeting.

McFarlane claimed that Reagan later called him to okay the missile sale. But Reagan told an investigating board that he could not remember such a phone call and did not know if he approved the shipments before or after they were sent.

At any rate, in late August 1985, Israel shipped almost one hundred TOW missiles to Iran—but no hostages were released by Muslim groups in Lebanon in response. Ghorbanifar, the Iranian go-between, then claimed that the delivery had been made to the wrong people in Iran. He told the Israe-

lis that Iran wanted another four hundred missiles but would release only one hostage in return.

How could Reagan agree to such a one-sided deal with a government that had been guilty of international terrorism, particularly when he was denouncing Iran in his public statements? Why didn't he ask who the moderates were or what Israel's motives were? After all, he had clashed with Israel before about policies in Lebanon. Still Reagan decided to go along with the plan. "The truth is, once we had information from Israel that we could trust the people in Iran, I didn't have to think thirty seconds about saying yes to their proposal," he said.[7]

The day after the second shipment was made to Iran, one American hostage, the Reverend Benjamin Weir, a Presbyterian minister, was released in Beirut.

By then, even McFarlane was deeply worried, particularly when the Iranians demanded another four hundred missiles. Working with McFarlane on these trades was Lieutenant Colonel Oliver North, the same man who had been involved in aiding the Contras. Although McFarlane was growing discouraged, North was enthusiastic about the negotiations and took control of getting a new shipment of HAWK

With the help of the Israelis, the Reagan administration swapped missiles for hostages in a deal with the Iranian leader Ayatollah Ruholla Khomeini, pictured here in Tehran. In a statement later, Reagan said he did not remember authorizing the deal.

(homing all-the-way killer) antiaircraft missiles on its way to Iran. North also brought private arms dealers into the arrangement.

The first shipment of HAWKs was completely bungled. Iran received only eighteen missiles, which turned out to be outmoded and obsolete. The Iranians wanted their money back, and of course, once again, no hostages were released.

By December McFarlane was depressed and exhausted. His grand plans for opening up Iran to the West had fallen apart. He had arranged for only one hostage to be released. He submitted his resignation, and Reagan accepted it, appointing McFarlane's chief aide, John Poindexter, to replace him. But even though McFarlane was not working day-to-day in the White House, he still served as a consultant on the Iran project.

Reagan's cabinet continued to object to the arms shipments to Iran. At a meeting on December 7, 1985, Shultz and Weinberger told the president flatly to drop the program. Shultz pointed out that working with Iran violated the policy Reagan himself had set—that the United States would not make deals with terrorists. He also told Reagan that other moderate Arab countries would be angry that the United States was working with right-wing groups like those in Iran.

Weinberger contended that the deals violated various U.S. laws. It was also possible, he said, that Iran would try to blackmail the United States because the Iranians knew that Reagan would not want the arms-for-hostages deal to become public.

A CIA official at the meeting also told Reagan that it was foolish to think that the United States was helping the moderates in Iran, because there were no moderates left in that country; they had all been killed by Khomeini. Even Donald Regan told

Reagan he had objections, although he was not as outspoken as the others.

But Reagan wanted to press ahead. He publicly denied that the U.S. government was trading arms for hostages or negotiating with terrorists. He preferred to view the situation another way. If my child is kidnapped, he said, "if I can find out that there is someone who has access to the kidnapper and can get my child back without doing anything for the kidnapper, I'd sure do that. And it would be perfectly fitting for me to reward that individual if he got my child back."[8]

The bizarre negotiations continued. McFarlane and North flew to London to meet with Iranian representatives, and North came back with a new plan that got the White House more deeply tangled in the deal. North proposed that the United States drop Israel from the arrangement and sell arms directly to Iran using weapons dealers he had worked with before in arming the Contras. This move ended the pretext that Israel was running the arms trades.

Although Reagan had promised his cabinet he would move slowly in the matter, he had already signed a "finding," a presidential authorization for covert action, for Poindexter. The finding gave presidential approval to the previous arms shipments; he signed two more in the next few weeks approving new shipments, including some sales by the United States to arms dealer Richard Secord, who would then sell the weapons to Iran. It was all part of the plan recommended by North.

The only Reagan cabinet member who was pushing strongly for the deal was William Casey, head of the Central Intelligence Agency. Weinberger and Shultz fought against the sales, but after Reagan signed orders that the United States rather than Israel would conduct the arms deals, they no longer tried to stop the plan. Nor did they resign in protest. "Instead they simply distanced themselves from the program," investigators later said.[9] Weinberger also released weapons to the CIA that he must have known would go to Iran.

In February the flow of U.S. TOW missiles began to Iran. Five hundred of them were delivered in mid-February; another five hundred were shipped to Iran at the end of February. But no hostages were released. Secord, however, was making millions in profits on the sales, some of which North was using to supply arms to the Contras.

All the while he was shipping arms to Iran, Reagan publicly denounced international terrorism. In April 1986 he even sent air force and navy planes to bomb Tripoli and Benghazi in Libya. The bombings were supposedly in retaliation against Libyan leader Muammar al-Qaddafi; the Reagan administration held Qaddafi responsible for the bombing of a German disco where an American military man had been killed. The U.S. bombs dropped on Libya killed many civilians, including Qaddafi's daughter.

In late May, Oliver North and Robert McFarlane traveled to Tehran, Iran, in an Israeli plane loaded with spare parts for HAWK missiles. It was an extremely dangerous idea—the two could have been taken hostage themselves. But McFarlane expected that Lebanese hostages would be freed soon after they arrived and that he could negotiate with top Iranian officials. Neither of those things happened, however. The Iranians they met made more and more demands, and McFarlane grew angrier and angrier. North wanted to send another shipment of HAWK spare parts to Iran, but McFarlane refused. They soon left Tehran with nothing accomplished. When Reagan heard that the mission had failed, he wrote in his diary: "It was a heartbreaking disappointment for all of us."[10]

In April 1986, the United States bombed Tripoli and
Benghazi, Libya. The Reagan administration stated that the
attacks were in retaliation against Libyan leader Muammar
al-Qaddafi (center), whom it held responsible for killing
an American military man in Germany.

Flying home, North told McFarlane not to be too upset; at least the arms deals were providing money to supply the Contras. McFarlane was surprised to hear this, but he assumed that Poindexter and Ronald Reagan knew all about it.

Finally, on July 26, 1986, the Muslims in Lebanon freed one hostage—Father Lawrence Martin Jenco, former head of Catholic Relief Services in Lebanon. But in the fall, three more Americans were kidnapped in Lebanon. The same pattern was repeated later in the fall: five hundred TOW missiles were shipped to Iran, one hostage was freed, and three more Americans were kidnapped. Instead of providing Muslim groups with a reason to release hostages, Reagan's deals with Iran had given them a new reason to kidnap Americans.

CHAPTER FIFTEEN
ON HIS WATCH

November 1986 proved a dismal month for the Reagan White House. Things had begun well enough: the Muslims in Beirut had released an American hostage, David Jacobsen, on November 2; Reagan had been pleased about that and believed that more hostages might be released soon, even though the Lebanese Muslim terrorists had already replaced those they freed by kidnapping more Americans.

But then, on November 4, Reagan suffered a significant defeat at the polls. Democrats recaptured control of the U.S. Senate by winning nine seats formerly held by Republicans and losing only one of their own. Reagan had campaigned hard for many Republican candidates but had been unable to stem the tide. Even though he had won a landslide victory in 1984, like most presidents he found it impossible to hold on to the gains of his party during midterm elections.

Meanwhile, a more serious crisis was brewing. The day before the election, *Al-Shiraa,* a Lebanese newspaper, reported that the United States had been selling arms to Iran in return for hostages and even described the visit that Robert McFarlane had made to Iran in May. By the day after the election,

Former hostages David Jacobsen, Rev. Lawrence Martin Jenco, and Rev. Benjamin Weir embrace in London in November 1986. While Americans were happy the men were free, many were troubled that the Reagan administration had bargained for their release.

American reporters knew about the story and were clamoring to find out more details. Had Jacobsen really been released because the United States had traded something to Iran?

Reagan and those on his staff who knew what was going on tried not to answer any of the questions. The president still had hopes that somehow more hostages might be released.

"I wanted to keep quiet about the events in Iran and Beirut, not because they were something I was ashamed of—getting out three hostages was something I was proud of—but because I didn't want anything to interfere with the impending release of the other hostages or to endanger the Iranians who were helping us," Reagan said.[1]

For the next few days Reagan lied about the situation and kept on lying while telling himself that his lies would help the hostages in Lebanon. He had done something he had sworn never to do: he had negotiated with terrorists. And those terrorists had outsmarted him. It seems to have been very difficult for him to face those facts. Even though hope that more hostages might be released was rapidly disappearing, he continued to think that perhaps everything would turn out all right in the end.

On November 7 Reagan appeared in the White House Rose Garden with the newly returned hostage and told reporters that Jacobsen had been released as the result of negotiations by a British emissary, Terry Waite. He also implied that whatever had gone on had the approval of Secretary of State George Shultz and Defense Secretary Caspar Weinberger—both of whom had *opposed* the arms-for-hostages deal.

At a national security group meeting with the president, John Poindexter tried to persuade cabinet members to support the dealings with Iran.

Shultz was increasingly angry about all this. "President Reagan, in his desire to free the hostages, had allowed himself to be sold a bill of goods," Shultz later said. "Poindexter had fabricated a high-toned rationale for a sordid swap, and the president had accepted it."[2]

On November 13, Reagan tried to explain his position more clearly to the American people. In a TV address he said that the arms deals they had heard about had been part of a plan to build up a new relationship with Iran and that such a friendship could help keep the Middle East from falling under Soviet control. He seemed angry and defensive to many who watched him, and he seemed to blame the press for exaggerating the story. He insisted that the United States had done little more than transfer small shipments of arms to Iran. But his speech was loaded with lies and inaccuracies—many of them based on a report given to Reagan by John Poindexter. For example, Reagan told the TV audience that all the parts and weapons supplied to Iran could have "easily fit into a single cargo plane."[3]

And he closed with a statement that many people found hard to understand: "We did not, repeat, did not trade weapons or anything else for hostages, nor will we."[4] If he wasn't trading arms for hostages, what was he doing? Americans asked themselves.

Clearly "the great communicator" was not getting his point across. Polls taken after the broadcast showed that most people opposed shipping arms to Iran and did not believe Reagan's version of the events. "For the first time, the president had gone before the American people to make his case and try to clear things up, and they had not believed him," Shultz said.[5]

In the next few days Reagan continued to depend heavily on Poindexter, North, and McFarlane for his information. Even Donald Regan had growing doubts about the truthfulness of these men, but he did not express them to the president. A disastrous news conference was held on November 19. During this session Reagan tried to answer questions from reporters, again basing his responses on information he had received from Poindexter. Reagan made many misstatements, partly because much of what Poindexter had told him was inconsistent with what Reagan already knew. Casey and Poindexter then went before a congressional committee a few days later and told several lies about the shipments to Iran.

Finally, under continuing pressure from Shultz, the president agreed that Attorney General Edwin Meese should make an inquiry into the affair. But Meese moved too slowly, and too much advance warning was given to Casey, North, and Poindexter about the upcoming investigation. At some interviews with the men involved, Meese did not even take notes or have a witness present. Meese later claimed that he did not suspect that he was investigating criminal activity at first; he thought he was merely trying to reconcile opposing points of view about what had happened.

Because of the advance warning, North was able to shred documents containing incriminating information. He and Casey were particularly worried that the press would find out about the link between the Iran arms sales and the supplies sent to the Contras. In spite of their cover-up efforts, however, one of Meese's assistants did find a memo which explained that from $10 million to $20 million of the money from the arms sales had gone to buy supplies for the Contras. Throughout this investigation, Reagan asked very few questions of Meese.

In late November, Meese reported to Reagan that the situation was much more questionable than he had at first expected. The United States had charged Iran $30 million for what amounted to $12 million in arms. Exactly where all the profits had gone was a mystery, but at least part of the money had gone to the Contras. Reagan's face grew white and pale; to those who were present at the meeting with Meese, the president seemed shocked and almost unable to speak. "My first reaction was that Poindexter and North wouldn't do anything like that without telling me—that there had to be a mistake," Reagan said.[6]

But no, there had been no mistake, and Meese told Reagan the situation was so serious that he would have to appoint a special review board, made up of both Democratic and Republican members, to investigate. Furthermore, Poindexter and North had to go. Although Reagan fired the two, he was still unable to fully accept the truth. When he spoke to North and gave him the bad news, he even called North a hero.

The next day Reagan announced that Poindexter and North had been fired, and Meese told the press about what had happened to the money that had come from selling arms to Iran. Some of what Meese said was inaccurate; he claimed that was because he still did not know the whole truth. But Reagan then went on television to say that he had asked two former senators, John Tower and Edmund Muskie, and former White House National Security Adviser Brent Scowcroft, to investigate the affair. A special independent prosecutor, Lawrence Walsh, was appointed a few weeks later.

The next few weeks were troubled ones at the White House as the press speculated about how much Reagan had known about the diversion of money to the Contras. Perhaps he had been told about it, some reporters said, but had not understood the full meaning of supplying the Contras. Perhaps he had given his approval without understanding that the program was illegal. Perhaps he had forgotten what staff members told him at various times. His hearing problems seemed to be getting worse; perhaps he had not even heard Poindexter telling him about the funds going to the Contras.

Eventually Poindexter testified that he had never told the president about the diversion, and no memo or document agreeing to that plan was ever found that Reagan had signed. Poindexter said he had destroyed such documents like the finding authorizing covert action. So Reagan's claim that he had known nothing about the funds for the Contras could not be refuted. But the questions in the minds of Americans have not gone away. Where did Reagan's lies end and the truth begin?

The turmoil continued. Congress announced that it, too, would investigate the Iran-Contra affair.

Reagan continued to blame the press for much of what was going on. He wasn't depressed or anxious, he insisted, but he was feeling "frustrated." "For the first time in my life, people didn't believe me. I had told the truth, but they still didn't believe me."[7]

His integrity had never been questioned before, but the American people didn't seem to trust him any more. All the goodwill he had built up with the nation had been washed away.

The clamor over the Iran-Contra affair would not end, and some of Reagan's strongest opponents in Congress even suggested that, depending on how deeply Reagan was involved, he might be impeached.

To his staff he seemed confused and forgetful. When he appeared before the Tower investigative board, he did not give very clear answers about his role in the Iran-Contra affair. He was unsure of when he had given approval for the arms shipments to Iran. Had he or had he not objected when McFarlane first told him about the shipments? The board concluded, based on McFarlane's testimony, that Reagan had given approval back in August 1985.

Had the president ever heard about the diversion of money to the Contras? He didn't think so, but he wasn't sure. The board found no evidence that he had heard about the Contra supplies. But the American people felt that he should have known and he should have stopped it.

The Tower board said Reagan had done a poor job of managing staff members and had relied too much on others in making decisions.

Staff members around Reagan believed that he had to clean house and get rid of more of the people involved in the Iran-Contra affair. North, Poindexter, and McFarlane were gone, but William Casey should be fired as well, staff members said. After all, he was closely involved in many decisions regarding the arms shipments and secret aid to the Contras. But questions about Casey's job ended in mid-December when he became seriously ill. He suffered a seizure just before going to testify before a Senate committee, and he was diagnosed with brain cancer. In late January he was forced to resign because of his illness. A few months later he died, leaving unanswered many questions about the Iran-Contra affair.

Some of Reagan's advisers and his wife, Nancy, believed that he had to fire his chief of staff, Donald Regan, as well. "Maybe this was unfair of me, but to some extent I blamed him [Donald Regan] for what had happened," Nancy Reagan said. "He was the chief of staff, and if he didn't know, I thought he should have."[8]

After all, Nancy Reagan pointed out, Regan liked to boast that a sparrow couldn't fly through the White House without his hearing it.

Regan fought to keep his job, and Reagan was at first hesitant to fire him. But the Tower board had singled Regan out for special criticism. He had a powerful role in the White House and was very much involved in the Iran meetings, the board found. "He, as much as anyone, should have insisted that an orderly process be observed," the board's final report said.[9]

That was the final blow. Regan agreed to leave, and Reagan brought in Howard Baker, former senator from Tennessee, to serve as his chief of staff. Baker was a wise choice, a man who did much, along with some other new staff members, to get the White House back on course.

When the Tower report was released at the end of February 1987, one of its most damaging conclusions was that, regardless of what Reagan thought of the situation, he did indeed trade arms for hostages. A group of Reagan's advisers believed that in light of the report, he had to admit to the American people that he had lied and he had to apologize. Even John Tower, who had served on the board, urged Reagan to do so. The future of the presidency was at stake. If Reagan should fail to satisfy Americans' questions about the affair, he might still be vulnerable to impeachment.

So on March 4 he went on television and told America: "A few months ago I told the American people I did not trade arms for hostages. My heart and my best intentions still tell me that's true, but the facts and the evidence tell me it is not. . . . There are reasons why it happened but no excuses. It was a mistake."[10]

Reagan would later backtrack on this apology

and insist again that he had not traded arms for hostages. In his memoirs he argued that he had been trying to open up relationships with moderate Iranians. He had trusted others to obey the law in doing so, he said, but they had not. Overnight after Reagan's speech his opinion ratings rose dramatically in the polls. Americans approved of the speech and of Reagan's apology for the Iran-Contra affair. "But that never made me feel as happy as some people might think it would," he said. "It was as if Americans were forgiving me for something I hadn't done."[11]

The investigation by Congress continued. As various members of Reagan's staff were interviewed by congressional committees during mid-1987, more questions arose about how Reagan could have embarked on such a disastrous scheme. As McFarlane, Poindexter and North testified, their stories conflicted with Reagan's version of the events. Who was telling the truth? Americans wanted to know. Poindexter tried to protect the president by denying that Reagan knew about the diversion of funds to the Contras. North, however, stressed that Reagan knew about his illegal activities and approved of everything. To many television viewers, North appeared courageous and patriotic with his flamboyant and defiant approach to Congress.

Eventually in March 1988, the special prosecutor, Lawrence Walsh, indicted North, Poindexter, and others involved in the Iran-Contra affair. Some pleaded guilty and some were convicted of various crimes. But some convictions were overturned because of their immunized testimony before Congress. During his trial in 1990, Poindexter reversed himself and insisted that Reagan had known about all the details of the Iran-Contra program. Reagan appeared in a videotaped interview during Poindexter's trial and denied such knowledge. To those who saw the tape, he seemed confused and forgetful.

Defense Secretary Caspar Weinberger was indicted as well for his role in covering up the affair afterward, but he was pardoned by President George Bush who succeeded Reagan in the White House.

Lawrence Walsh's final report on the affair was not released until 1994. In it he contended that most senior officials in the Reagan and Bush administrations had lied in their attempts to avoid taking blame for the scandal.

Most of the problems arising from the Iran-Contra affair ended for Reagan with the conclusion of the congressional hearings. His term was almost completed, and House and Senate members seemed hesitant to create national upheaval by attempting to punish Reagan in some way. Perhaps that was because few members of Congress wanted to endure another investigation like the Watergate hearings that drove President Richard Nixon out of office. Or perhaps it was because Reagan was about to leave the White House anyway.

At the time it seemed that Reagan's presidency was finished. His reputation with many Americans had been seriously tarnished; his ability to handle crises seemed impaired; his power to deal with Congress had eroded. It seemed that all he could do with his remaining time in office was sit and wait for his term to end. But there was more to come; some of the most lasting impact of the Reagan presidency would be achieved in the days ahead.

CHAPTER SIXTEEN
BREAKING DOWN WALLS

In June 1987, just after attending an economic summit in Italy, Reagan flew to West Berlin. There he stood at the Brandenburg Gate, before tens of thousands of West Berliners. The gate marked the dividing line between free West Germany and Communist-controlled East Germany. Behind him stood the huge reinforced concrete panels of the Berlin Wall, a barrier built in the 1960s to keep East Berliners from escaping to the freedom of the West. The western side of the wall was plastered with graffiti and slogans and artwork expressing the hope of Germans for the eventual liberation of the East.

It was an inspiring moment for Reagan, and he could not pass up the chance to tell the world about the differences between Communist-controlled Europe and the free West. He also challenged the leader of the Soviet Union, Mikhail Gorbachev, to make changes: "General Secretary Gorbachev, if you seek peace, if you seek prosperity for the Soviet Union and Eastern Europe, if you seek liberalization: Come here to this gate! Mr. Gorbachev, open this gate! Mr. Gorbachev, tear down this wall."[1]

In only three years, the wall would tumble down, and although Reagan would no longer be president, he could well claim credit for having a role in changing the landscape of Europe.

For many people it was truly amazing that Reagan, of all presidents, should eventually play such a great part in extending a hand in friendship to the Soviet Union. During his career in politics, Reagan had long taken a firm line against communism. He truly believed that the Soviet Union would do almost anything to advance its goal of world conquest. After being elected president, he had fought for building the military might of the United States to keep up with the huge military machine of the Soviet Union.

In December 1981, during his first term, he had spoken out against the Soviet Union when it imposed martial law on Poland, where the Solidarity labor movement threatened to overthrow the Communist government. In 1983, Reagan had shocked many Americans by delivering a speech that strongly condemned the Soviets. "Let us be aware," he had said, "that while they [the Soviets] preach the supremacy of the state, declare its omnipotence over individual man, and predict its eventual domination of all peoples on the earth, they are the focus of evil in the modern world."[2]

It would be a big mistake, he said, to say that the United States and the Soviet Union were equally at fault for the nuclear arms race. The world could not ignore the aggression of the Soviet Union, which he labeled "an evil empire."[3]

The Soviets responded by comparing Reagan to Hitler. It seemed that the two sides could never be further apart.

In addition, Reagan had rejected all pleas from members of the U.S. antinuclear movement who wanted the nation to make concessions to the Soviets regarding arms reductions.

But despite the fact that many liberals believed Reagan was a warmonger, anxious to push a button that could destroy his enemies, he claimed that he feared nuclear war and yearned to rid the world of such weapons. He objected to the concept of nuclear deterrence—the idea that each superpower would build up a huge war chest of nuclear arms and thereby keep the other side too frightened to make war. The policy was often referred to as "mutual assured destruction," or MAD. As Reagan said, "It was like having two westerners standing in a saloon aiming their guns at each other's heads—permanently."[4]

Reagan preferred to cut back the weapons on both sides and eventually eliminate them. Some in the Pentagon objected to his ideas, he said: "They tossed around macabre jargon about 'throw weights' and 'kill ratios' as if they were talking about baseball scores. But for the eight years I was president I never let my dream of a nuclear-free world fade from my mind."[5]

Even so, for several years during his presidency, there was conflict between some officials in his administration, like George Shultz and George Bush, who wanted to negotiate with the Russians for nuclear arms reductions, and others, like Caspar Weinberger, who wanted to maintain a strong nuclear arsenal as a way to deter the Soviet Union from aggression. Nancy Reagan favored negotiations with the Soviet Union and was a strong voice for reaching out to the other side.

Other presidents before Reagan had held summits and arms talks with the Soviets. For example, President Jimmy Carter and Soviet leader Leonid Brezhnev had signed a Strategic Arms Limitation Treaty known as SALT II, designed to limit the number of nuclear arms each superpower could build. Although both nations had supposedly been voluntarily abiding by the treaty, it had never been ratified by the U.S. Senate, and Reagan found it objectionable. He thought that the Soviet Union was not abiding strictly by the limits. In addition, the United States had developed a new missile-firing submarine that would violate the treaty if the United States did not remove other nuclear submarines from service.

Furthermore, Reagan believed that the whole idea of the treaty was flawed, that it tended to encourage both nations to build up nuclear forces to the limits set by the treaty. He would have preferred, he said, to reduce the number of weapons that both sides already owned.

Reagan had another idea, too: why not set up some kind of non-nuclear defensive system to shoot down enemy nuclear missiles before they even hit the United States?

Various military officials had from time to time thought about such a system, but no one had ever gotten very far with the concept. It became a dream Reagan refused to give up.

Early in 1983, Reagan proposed the idea to the Joint Chiefs of Staff, who agreed it was worth investigating. Without waiting for much scientific or military analysis of the concept, Reagan plunged ahead in March and announced to the American public what he had in mind. "Wouldn't it be better to save lives than to avenge them?" he asked. "Are we not capable of demonstrating our peaceful intentions by applying all our abilities and our ingenuity to achieving a truly lasting stability?"[6]

Although many Americans believed the idea was worth investigating, many others, particularly scientists, were aghast. The nation, they said, could spend billions on this program, which was little more than an idea out of a science-fiction novel, and end up with nothing. Reagan and others countered with their belief that there was nothing American ingenuity and know-how could not accomplish. Furthermore, they believed that the Soviets had already begun research on such an idea. At any rate, Congress did appropriate funds to research the idea, officially known as the Strategic Defense Initiative, but often referred to as "Star Wars."

During Reagan's first administration, the Soviet Union had three different leaders. Reagan corresponded with them, but little or no progress was made toward world peace. But shortly after Reagan's second term began, a new, younger leader who favored arms control—Mikhail Gorbachev— took over. Reagan invited him to join in a summit conference in the United States.

Letters went back and forth between the two, and in November 1985 they met for the first time in Geneva, Switzerland. The scene of the summit was a beautiful twenty-room château on the shore of Lake Geneva.

The two men began by stating their differences. The United States was paranoid about the Soviet Union, Gorbachev said. The Soviets wanted only peace, not war.

Reagan objected to the way the Soviets interfered with the economy inside their country, and he raised questions about what some called Soviet imperialism—moves to ensure Communist rule in countries outside Russia. In particular, Reagan denounced the invasion of Afghanistan, where the Soviets were trying to reinforce an unpopular Communist government. He criticized abuses of human rights inside the U.S.S.R., and he questioned the Soviet Union's refusal to allow Soviet dissidents to emigrate to other countries.

Gorbachev objected to the Strategic Defense Initiative, which he said could start an arms race in space. Reagan responded that if Americans could develop an effective defensive system against nuclear arms, they would share their knowledge with the Russians.

Yet despite their disagreements, the two did like each other. Throughout his political career, Reagan had always believed that if he could just talk with the leader of the Soviet Union alone, one-on-one, he could explain how Americans felt and how their system worked. He believed he could convince the Soviet leader of the value of democracy and the American way of life. It may have been a naive idea, but Reagan's faith in himself and in the power of his wit and personality played a big part in the talks at Geneva.

One afternoon the two walked down to the château's boathouse together, sat in front of a roaring fire with just their interpreters present, and talked about key issues. On their walk back, Reagan invited Gorbachev to a summit in the United States, and Gorbachev agreed but also invited Reagan to Moscow for a third summit.

At the summit's end, the two men announced their joint determination to curb the arms race and improve relations between their countries. They were fine goals, but lacking in substance. Nothing had been decided about SDI or about what the arms cuts might be. Still, the two men had begun a friendship that impressed the world.

In the letters they sent to each other after Geneva, Reagan and Gorbachev accomplished very little, although both proposed various cuts in nuclear weapons in Europe. Some Western European leaders were nervous, however, that the United States might be abandoning its commitment to defend Europe.

The real sticking point between Reagan and Gorbachev always seemed to be the Strategic Defense

Initiative. Reagan refused to discuss SDI, and that commitment made it difficult for Gorbachev to convince conservatives inside the Soviet Union that arms control was advantageous for the country. The Soviet hard-liners insisted that Star Wars had to go before the U.S.S.R. would reduce its defenses. For many Americans the discussion was frustrating. Why refuse to negotiate away a form of technology that no one might ever be able to develop? On the other hand, some American conservatives believed there must be something to SDI or the Soviets wouldn't be afraid of it.

Despite their differences the two men agreed to hold a second summit in Reykjavík, Iceland, in October 1986, although they seemed so far apart in their proposals that many feared that little would be accomplished.

In Reykjavík, Gorbachev proposed that both sides cut back long-range ballistic missiles by half while working on eliminating them completely over ten years. Meanwhile, any research on SDI must be confined strictly to the laboratory for ten years. Reagan responded by offering to eliminate all American ballistic missiles over ten years. At the end of that time the United States or the Soviet Union could set up an SDI system as insurance against cheating or accidents. Gorbachev then proposed eliminating all the world's nuclear weapons, including bombers and cruise missiles, in which the United States had an advantage, and ballistic missiles, in which the Soviets were ahead. The Soviets would also cut back their conventional forces. In return, Gorbachev said, Reagan must totally give up his dream of Star Wars except for laboratory research.

Reagan was furious and told Gorbachev that SDI was not something he would bargain away. He couldn't understand, he said, why the Soviets would keep objecting to this system when the Americans were willing to share the results of their research. He offered to open up U.S. laboratories and make the research available to the whole world. The problem with restricting SDI to the laboratory, he said, was that once lab research was over, it could take years to deploy, or install, an SDI system. While installation was going on, any enemy nation, knowing the United States had cut back its nuclear forces, could press a button and send a missile into the United States.

Gorbachev would not budge, and neither would Reagan. "The meeting is over," Reagan snapped at Secretary of State George Shultz. "Let's go George, we're leaving."[7] The stunned Soviets tried to get Reagan to stay another day, but he refused. His mind was made up.

At first the American people were shocked, too. All the high hopes for an arms control agreement had been smashed. But later, both Reagan and Gorbachev insisted they were not finished talking and that progress had been made. Eventually Gorbachev backtracked and argued there should be a treaty eliminating intermediate range U.S. and Soviet missiles in Europe regardless of what Reagan's plans were for SDI. Why did Gorbachev change his mind? Perhaps he had decided that SDI stood no chance of being developed anyway; perhaps he needed to come up with some version of an arms control agreement in order to keep political power in his own country.

Whatever Gorbachev's reasons were, Reagan was eager to move ahead as well because of his own political problems. By the middle of 1987 when these arms talks were growing more intense, he was deeply enmeshed in the Iran-Contra affair. Gorbachev's willingness to negotiate gave him a chance to take positive action and not merely defend himself against critics.

So throughout 1987 various government agencies and allies of the United States considered Gorbachev's proposal and issued their opinions. There were those who objected strongly to Reagan's move toward negotiating with the Soviets. Many New Right conservatives believed that Reagan had betrayed them and that he would greatly weaken the military defenses of the United States and Europe with these arms cutbacks.

In fall 1987 the Soviet foreign minister Eduard Shevardnadze and Secretary of State Shultz met and outlined terms for what came to be called the Intermediate Nuclear Forces, or INF, treaty. They also announced that Gorbachev would come to the United States in December for another summit.

When Gorbachev arrived in the United States, hopeful Americans welcomed him as the the man who was liberating the Soviet Union from old-style communism. Struck with "Gorby fever," they jammed the streets to cheer him as he rode by in a limousine. Gorbachev often stopped to shake hands with Americans. Scenes of Reagan and Gorbachev together on television warmed the hearts of Americans who were tired and fearful of the arms race. It seemed as if, finally, relations between the United States and the Soviet Union were thawing.

On December 8 the two men signed the treaty. It called for destruction over three years of more than 800 American and more than 1,800 Soviet nuclear missiles with a range of 300 to 3,400 miles.

In their private meetings at this summit, however, few if any other new agreements were made. Publicly the two men basked in the glow of flash bulbs and TV lights. They had accomplished something no other leaders of the U.S.S.R. and the

Reagan and Soviet leader Mikhail Gorbachev shake hands
after signing a historic disarmament treaty in Washington,
D.C., on December 8, 1987.

United States had been able to do since the end of World War II. The positive publicity helped shield both men from other problems engulfing their nations. The people of the Soviet Union were pleased that their government would start putting money into producing consumer goods instead of weapons. In the United States it was difficult for senators and representatives to attack Reagan for his poor leadership in the Iran-Contra affair when he had scored this magnificent achievement with Gorbachev. Economic problems were building up in the United States as well. In October the stock market had its largest one-day collapse of prices since 1914, but the summit in Washington distracted many from that.

In May 1988, Reagan went to Moscow to see Gorbachev. The walls of communism had crumbled even further by then. Gorbachev had announced he would pull Soviet troops out of Afghanistan, and he made plans to change the Soviet economy by introducing principles of capitalism and individual ownership.

Reagan had hoped they could sign another treaty in Moscow to plan cutbacks in intercontinental ballistic missiles, the giant long-range nuclear missiles that the two countries had aimed at each other. But their differences on these arms were too great. START, the Strategic Arms Reduction Treaty, involving these weapons was not signed until George Bush became president.

In Moscow, the Soviet people gave Reagan the same warm welcome as the Americans had given Gorbachev. Crowds lined the streets to cheer as Reagan drove by. "On the streets of Moscow, looking into thousands of faces," Reagan said, "I was reminded once again that it's not people who make war, but governments—and people deserve governments that fight for peace in the nuclear age."[8]

A highlight of the trip occured when the Reagans and the Gorbachevs attended a performance of the Bolshoi Ballet together. Standing at attention, the audience listened to "The Star-Spangled Banner" ringing out before the performance. This dramatic moment touched Ronald Reagan deeply. He and Gorbachev had forged a powerful agreement that could make the world a safer place.

EPILOGUE

Finally the Reagan era was ending. After the inauguration ceremonies, the newly elected president, George Bush, and his wife, Barbara, walked with the Reagans down the steps of the Capitol to where a marine helicopter was waiting for the outgoing president. Nancy Reagan broke away briefly to hug a Secret Service man who was there to say good-bye. Then as he stood on the steps of the helicopter while television cameras caught the scene, Reagan turned and saluted Bush, who returned the salute.

Ronald Reagan returned to California. Despite his failings and mistakes, he was leaving office buoyed by the love and affection of his fellow citizens. He had accomplished much and brought about great changes in American life.

Among other things, he had brought about a drive to deregulate much of American business, had changed and reformed the tax structure and poured billions into the nation's defense system. He had persuaded Congress to do his bidding, appointed numerous conservative judges, and taken aggressive actions that at times mired him in deep controversy.

For better or worse, Reagan would go down in history as a president who was determined to change the course of American government and business. Some believed that Congress had prevented him from making as many positive changes as he would have, had it not been for the obstacles the legislature created; others believed that the Reagan era was a disaster and that, had it not been for Congress, Reagan would have done a great deal more damage than he did. Some objected that his administration's policies of deregulation removed the checks on business and made possible the greed and excessive profit-taking of the 1980s. Others criticized him for having cut the funding for social programs designed to help the poor while, because of a loyalty to defense contractors, particularly in California, he fattened the defense budget. Many working people were outraged that the Reagan administration in its eagerness to free business from constraints had knocked the teeth out of many labor laws that for decades had empowered American workers to strike for adequate pay and benefits. Still others argued generally that Reagan's policies enabled the rich to get richer at the expense of people in the middle and lower classes.

Many could not forget the stain left on the Reagan presidency by the Iran-Contra affair. Investigations into the affair, court proceedings, and criminal convictions related to it continued for years after Reagan was out of office, all at the expense of the taxpayers. As new evidence came to bear, and with the report issued in January 1994 by the independent counsel, Lawrence Walsh, it became apparent that Reagan and others in his administration knew more about illegal activities and were much more deeply involved in them than they ever admitted. It was also revealed that the Bush administration obstructed the investigation into the affair.

Still, Reagan had made impressive changes in the face of the world. Together with Mikhail Gorbachev of the Soviet Union, he had walked toward a peace that some believed would be the greatest in

A homeless man passes by a fashionable eatery during the late 1980s. Some look back on the Reagan era as a time of prosperity; others remember it as a time when the gap between the rich and poor widened, the middle class took on additional tax burdens, and the national debt increased manyfold.

the history of the world. It was true, of course, that the Soviet Union might have headed in that direction no matter who was president. But Reagan was quick to rise to the challenge and to accept the peacemaking overtures from Gorbachev, and he deserves credit at least for that.

In many ways, Reagan left office just before he would have had to answer for some of his questionable policies. The extent to which members of his administration and the president himself were embroiled in Iran-Contra, shady dealings that brought about the savings and loan crisis, the Wedtech affair, and other scandals that plagued the Reagan era took time to come to light, and many of the allegations still have not been proved. Problems created by Reagan's deregulation policies and changes in the tax laws remained to be solved. Also, once the Reagan administration left Washington, it became clear that what had seemed to be prosperity during the 1980s was really a spending spree and that suddenly the country, burdened with an enormous financial debt, was headed for a recession. That recession, inherited by Reagan's successor, would help defeat George Bush in his bid for reelection in 1992.

Strangely, when looking back at the political career of Ronald Reagan and all the accomplishments and failings of his administration, many if not most Americans remember him fondly. They recall the confidence and pride they felt as they listened to "the great communicator" deliver his message to the people. They remember low unemployment and low inflation. They remember his sense of humor and his jousting with his challengers. For many, the Reagan era was a period of good feeling and prosperity; others consider it an era of government deceit that contributed greatly to a sharp downturn in the quality of American life in the 1990s. The truth is not only for historians but for all of us to decide.

In 1988, after eight years in the White House, the former president and first lady retired to their 688-acre mountain ranch near Santa Barbara, California.

SOURCE NOTES

Chapter 1
1. Ronald Reagan, *An American Life* (New York: Simon & Schuster, 1990), p. 21.
2. Ibid., p. 27.
3. Ibid., p. 25.
4. Anne Edwards, *Early Reagan: The Rise to Power* (New York: William Morrow, 1987), p. 58.
5. Reagan, *An American Life,* p. 35.
6. Edwards, *Early Reagan,* p. 69.
7. Reagan, *An American Life,* p. 48.

Chapter 2
1. Reagan, *An American Life,* p. 64.
2. Ibid., p. 64.
3. Ibid., p. 76.
4. Ibid., p. 79.

Chapter 3
1. Ibid., p. 89.
2. Edwards, *Early Reagan,* p. 171.
3. Ronald Reagan and Richard Hubler, *Where's the Rest of Me?* (New York: Dell, 1965), p. 96.
4. Laurence Leamer, *Make-Believe: The Story of Nancy and Ronald Reagan* (New York: Harper & Row, 1983), p. 105.

5. Reagan, *An American Life,* p. 91.
6. Ibid., p. 92.
7. Ibid., p. 96.

Chapter 4
1. Reagan, *An American Life,* p. 115.
2. Edwards, *Early Reagan,* p. 355.
3. Nancy Reagan with William Novak, *My Turn: The Memoirs of Nancy Reagan* (New York: Dell, 1989), p. 99.
4. Hedrick Smith, Adam Clymer, Leonard Silk, Robert Lindsey, Richard Burt, *Reagan: The Man, the President* (New York: Macmillan, 1980), p. 34.

Chapter 5
1. Nancy Reagan, *My Turn,* p. 129.
2. Ronald Reagan, *An American Life,* p. 127.
3. Ibid., p. 129.
4. Ibid., p. 136.
5. Ronald Reagan, *Speaking My Mind: Selected Speeches* (New York: Simon & Schuster, 1989), p. 26.
6. Ibid., p. 36.
7. Haynes Johnson, *Sleepwalking Through History: America in the Reagan Years* (New York: W. W. Norton, 1991), p. 69.
8. Ronald Reagan, *An American Life,* p. 145.
9. Bill Boyarsky, *The Rise of Ronald Reagan* (New York: Random House, 1968), pp. 154-55.

Chapter 6
1. Nancy Reagan, *My Turn,* p. 138.
2. Kitty Kelley, *Nancy Reagan: The Unauthorized Biography* (New York: Simon & Schuster, 1991), p. 147.
3. Frank Van Der Linden, *The Real Reagan* (New York: William Morrow, 1981), p. 86.

SOURCE NOTES

4. Ronald Reagan, *An American Life,* p. 161.
5. James MacGregor Burns, *The Crosswinds of Freedom* (New York: Alfred Knopf, 1989), p. 396.
6. Johnson, *Sleepwalking Through History,* p. 79.
7. Ronald Reagan, *An American Life,* p. 180.
8. Boyarsky, *The Rise of Ronald Reagan,* p. 189.
9. Lou Cannon, *Ronnie and Jessie: A Political Odyssey* (New York: Doubleday, 1969), p. 178.
10. Nancy Reagan, *My Turn,* p. 139.
11. Ibid., p. 140.

Chapter 7
1. Cannon, *Ronnie and Jessie,* p. 263.
2. Ronald Reagan, *An American Life,* p. 178.
3. Lou Cannon, *Reagan* (New York: Putnam, 1982), p. 174.
4. Ibid., p. 180.
5. Ronald Reagan, *An American Life,* p. 190.
6. Cannon, *Reagan,* p. 185.

Chapter 8
1. Bob Schieffer and Gary Paul Gates, *The Acting President* (New York: E. P. Dutton, 1989), p. 59.
2. Ronald Reagan, *An American Life,* p. 195.
3. Cannon, *Reagan,* p. 211.
4. Ronald Reagan, *An American Life,* p. 201.
5. Cannon, *Reagan,* p. 215.
6. Nancy Reagan, *My Turn,* p. 208.
7. Michael Schaller, *Reckoning with Reagan: America and Its President in the 1980s* (New York: Oxford University Press, 1992), p. 17.
8. Nancy Reagan, *My Turn,* p. 209.

Chapter 9
1. Ronald Reagan, *An American Life,* p. 203.
2. Ibid., p. 207.
3. Cannon, *Reagan,* p. 239.

4. Edwin Meese III, *With Reagan: The Inside Story* (Washington, D.C.: Regnery Gateway, 1992), p. 11.
5. Cannon, *Reagan*, p. 239.
6. Nancy Reagan, *My Turn*, p. 215.
7. Ibid., p. 217.
8. Cannon, *Reagan*, p. 277.
9. Johnson, *Sleepwalking Through History*, p. 60.
10. Schieffer and Gates, *The Acting President*, p. 90.
11. Cannon, *Reagan*, p. 283.
12. Ibid., p. 295.
13. Ronald Reagan, *An American Life*, p. 221.
14. Cannon, *Reagan*, p. 297.

Chapter 10
1. Ronald Reagan, *An American Life*, p. 226.
2. Schieffer and Gates, *The Acting President*, p. 91.
3. Donald T. Regan, *For the Record: From Wall Street to Washington* (New York: Harcourt Brace Jovanovich, 1988), p. 267.
4. Ronald Reagan, *An American Life*, p. 232.
5. Lou Cannon, *President Reagan: The Role of a Lifetime* (New York: Simon & Schuster, 1991), p. 245.
6. Ibid., p. 241.
7. David A. Stockman, *The Triumph of Politics: Why the Reagan Revolution Failed* (New York: Harper & Row, 1986), p. 11.
8. Herbert L. Abrams, *The President Has Been Shot* (New York: Norton, 1992), p. 60.
9. Ibid., p. 62.
10. Ibid., p. 106.
11. Ibid., p. 188.
12. Ibid., p. 74.
13. Mark Hertsgaard, *On Bended Knee: The Press and the Reagan Presidency*, (New York: Schocken Books, 1989), p. 203.

SOURCE NOTES

14. Stockman, *The Triumph of Politics,* p. 13.
15. Ronald Reagan, *An American Life,* p. 337.

Chapter 11
1. Cannon, *President Reagan,* p. 401.
2. Ronald Reagan, *An American Life,* p. 428.
3. Cannon, *President Reagan,* p. 449.
4. Mark Hertsgaard, *On Bended Knee: The Press and the Reagan Presidency* (New York: Schocken Books, 1989), p. 212.

Chapter 12
1. Cannon, *President Reagan,* pp. 512-13.
2. Mark Hertsgaard, *On Bended Knee,* p. 258.
3. Nancy Reagan, *My Turn,* p. 275.
4. Ibid., p. 277.
5. Ibid., p. 278.
6. Ronald Reagan, *An American Life,* p. 328.
7. Nancy Reagan, *My Turn,* p. 278.
8. Cannon, *President Reagan,* p. 550.

Chapter 13
1. Cannon, *President Reagan,* p. 561.
2. Regan, *For the Record,* p. 281.
3. Ronald Reagan, *An American Life,* pp. 477-78.
4. U.S. House of Representatives Select Committee, *Report of the Congressional Committees Investigating the Iran-Contra Affair* (Washington, D.C.: U.S. Government Printing Office, 1987), p. 39.
5. Ronald Reagan, *An American Life,* p. 487.

Chapter 14
1. Cannon, *President Reagan,* p. 611.
2. Ibid., pp. 611-12.
3. Regan, *For the Record,* p. 21.
4. Ronald Reagan, *An American Life,* p. 505.

5. Ibid., p. 506.
6. Cannon, *President Reagan,* p. 616.
7. Ronald Reagan, *An American Life,* p. 506.
8. Ibid., p. 512.
9. Cannon, *President Reagan,* p. 641.
10. Ronald Reagan, *An American Life,* p. 528.

Chapter 15

1. Ronald Reagan, *An American Life,* p. 527.
2. George P. Shultz, *Turmoil and Triumph: My Years As Secretary of State* (New York: Scribner's, 1993), p. 814.
3. Cannon, *President Reagan,* p. 683.
4. Ronald Reagan, *An American Life,* p. 528.
5. Shultz, *Turmoil and Triumph,* p. 820.
6. Ronald Reagan, *An American Life,* p. 530.
7. Ibid., p. 532.
8. Nancy Reagan, *My Turn,* p. 331.
9. William S. Cohen and George J. Mitchell, *Men of Zeal: A Candid Inside Story of the Iran-Contra Hearings* (New York: Viking Press, 1988), p. 231.
10. Cannon, *President Reagan,* p. 736.
11. Ronald Reagan, *An American Life,* p. 541.

Chapter 16

1. Ronald Reagan, *An American Life,* p. 683.
2. Ibid., p. 570.
3. Ibid., p. 570.
4. Ibid., p. 547.
5. Ibid., p. 550.
6. Cannon, *President Reagan,* p. 332.
7. Ronald Reagan, *An American Life,* p. 679.
8. Ibid., p. 709.

BIBLIOGRAPHY

Boyarsky, Bill. *The Rise of Ronald Reagan.* New York: Random House, 1968.

Brown, Edmund G. (Pat), Sr. *Reagan and Reality: The Two Californias.* New York: Praeger, 1970.

Burns, James MacGregor. *The Crosswinds of Freedom.* New York: Alfred Knopf, 1989.

Cannon, Lou. *President Reagan: The Role of a Lifetime.* New York: Simon & Schuster, 1991.

————. *Reagan.* New York: Putnam, 1982.

————. *Ronnie and Jessie: A Political Odyssey.* New York: Doubleday, 1969.

Cockburn, Leslie. *Out of Control: The Story of the Reagan Administration's Secret War in Nicaragua, the Illegal Arms Pipeline, and the Contra Drug Connection.* New York: Viking Press, 1988.

Cohen, William S., and George J. Mitchell. *Men of Zeal: A Candid Inside Story of the Iran-Contra Hearings.* New York: Viking Press, 1988.

Edwards, Anne. *Early Reagan: The Rise to Power.* New York: William Morrow, 1987.

Johnson, Haynes. *Sleepwalking Through History: America in the Reagan Years.* New York: W. W. Norton, 1991.

Leamer, Laurence. *Make-Believe: The Story of Nancy and Ronald Reagan.* New York: Harper & Row, 1983.

Meese, Edwin, III. *With Reagan: The Inside Story.* Washington, D.C.: Regnery Gateway, 1992.

Reagan, Nancy, with William Novak. *My Turn.* New York: Dell, 1989.

Reagan, Ronald. *An American Life.* New York: Dell, 1989.

————. *Speaking My Mind: Selected Speeches.* New York: Simon & Schuster, 1989.

Reagan, Ronald, and Richard Hubler. *Where's the Rest of Me?* New York: Dell, 1965.

Regan, Donald T. *For the Record: From Wall Street to Washington.* New York: Harcourt Brace Jovanovich, 1988.

Schaller, Michael. *Reckoning with Reagan: America and Its President in the 1980s.* New York: Oxford University Press, 1992.

Schieffer, Bob, and Gary Paul Gates. *The Acting President.* New York: E. P. Dutton, 1989.

Shultz, George P. *Turmoil and Triumph: My Years As Secretary of State.* New York: Scribner's, 1993.

Stockman, David A. *The Triumph of Politics: Why the Reagan Revolution Failed.* New York: Harper & Row, 1986.

U.S. House of Representatives Select Committee to Investigate Covert Arms Transactions with Iran and U.S. Senate Select Committee on Secret Military Assistance to Iran and the Nicaraguan Opposition. *Report of the Congressional Committees Investigating the Iran-Contra Affair.* Washington, D.C.: U.S. Government Printing Office, 1987.

Van Der Linden, Frank. *The Real Reagan.* New York: William Morrow, 1981.

White, Theodore H. *America in Search of Itself: The Making of the President 1956-1980.* New York: Harper & Row, 1982.

Wills, Garry. *Reagan's America: Innocents at Home.* Garden City, N.Y.: Doubleday, 1987.

Index

Page numbers in *italics* indicate illustrations.

Abortion, 66–67, 107
Afghanistan, 164, 170
Aid to Families with Dependent Children, 74
Air controllers strike, 110
Al-Shiraa, 149
American Veterans Committee, 40
Anderson, John, 87, 90
Arms-for-hostages trade, 139–59
Arms reduction, 161–71
Astrology, 59, 130
Atlantic Monthly, 111
Ayres, Lew, 43

Baker, Howard, 87, 157
Baker, James, 99, 106, 130, 132
Beckel, Robert, 123
Bedtime for Bonzo, 45

Begin, Menachem, 115
Bergen-Belsen concentration camp, 129
Berlin Wall, 160
Birth of a Nation, The, 10
Bitburg cemetary, 128–29
Boland amendment, 134
Bonn, summit in, 128–29
Brady, James, 105
Brezhnev, Leonid, 162
Brother Rat, 32
Brother Rat and a Baby, 32
Brown, Edmund G., Sr., 51, 56–57, 66
Brown, Jerry, 69
Burns, James MacGregor, 63
Bush, Barbara, 172
Bush, George, 87, 88, 89, 90, 94, 105, 141, 159, 162, 170, 172, 175

Business, deregulation of, 102, 111, 112–13, 172, 173, 175

Cannon, Lou, 131
Carter, Jimmy, 84, 86, 87, 90–96, 162
Casey, William J., 90, 99, 134, 137, 145, 153, 156
Castro, Fidel, 119, 121
Catalina Island, 27
Cavalry, 25
Central Intelligence Agency (CIA), 134, 140
Chicago Cubs, 26–27
Christopher, George, 56
Clark, Judson, 77
Cleaver, Margaret, 14, 16, 25
Communism, 41. See also Soviet Union
Congress, 155, 158–59
Connally, John, 87
Conservatism, 86–87
Contras, diversion of money to, 154, 156
Crane, Philip, 87

Davis, Loyal, 44, 51
Davis, Nancy, 44–45, 46. See also Reagan, Nancy
Death penalty, 66
Death Valley Days, 52
Deaver, Michael, 88, 106, 129

Debates, presidential, 89, 95–96, 124–27
Deficit, 112–13
Democrats, 34, 51, 107, 149
Disciples of Christ, 10
Divorce, 43
Dixon, IL, 10
Dole, Robert, 83, 87
Donovan's Brain, 45

Eureka College, 16–19
Executive Club of Chicago, 80

Fahd, King (Saudi Arabia), 135
FBI, 41
Fibber McGee and Molly, 24
"Finding," 145
Football, 17–18
Ford, Gerald, 79, 82–83, 84, 94
Foreign affairs, 114–21
Fort Roach, 37–39
Frazer, B. J., 14
Free-market economy, 101
Friedman, Milton, 101

Gates, Gary Paul, 79
Gemayel, Bashir, 116
Geneva, Switzerland, 164–65
Gergen, David, 111
GE Theater, 49–52

Ghorbanifar, Manucher, 140, 141–42
Gipp, George, 34, 36
Goldwater, Barry, 52–54, 82, 86
Gorbachev, Mikhail, 160, 164–71, *169*, 173
Governor, Reagan as, 54–57
Great Depression, 19
Great Gildersleeve, The, 24
Grenada, 119

Habib, Philip, 115
Haig, Alexander, 99, 105–6, 116
Hakim, Albert, 135
Hal Roach Studios, 37
HAWK missiles, 143–44, 146
Hayakawa, S.I., 64
Hellcats of the Navy, 47, 51
Hinckley, John, 105
Holden, Ardis, 44, 45
Holden, Bill, 44, 45
Hollywood, 27–28
Hollywood Independent Citizens Committee of Arts, Sciences and Professions, 40
House Un-American Activities Committee, 41

Inflation, 122
Interest rates, 122

Intermediate Nuclear Force (INF) treaty, 168
Iowa, campaign in, 87–88
Iran, hostages in, 86, 139
Iran-Contra affair, 132–37, 173, 175
Israel, 115, 139–41, 145

Jacobsen, David, 149, *150*
Jenco, Rev. Lawrence Martin, 148, *150*
John Birch Society, 57
Johnny Belinda, 43
Johnson, Haynes, 93
Johnson, Lyndon, 53
Joint Chiefs of Staff, 118, 163
Junk bonds, 112

Kennedy, Robert F., 71
Kerr, Clark, 64
Khomeini, Ayatollah Ruholla, 139, *142*
Killers, The, 52
Kings Row, 36–37, 40
Knute Rockne, All American, 36, 40, 85
Kohl, Helmut, 129

Laffer, Albert, 101
Las Vegas nightclub act, 45–46, *47*
Laxalt, Paul, 109

Lebanon, 114, 115 "Let the People Rule" speech, 80
Libya, 114, 116
Little Brown Church in the Valley, 45
Love Is on the Air, 30
Lowell Park, 13, *15*
Luckett, Edith, 44

MacArthur, Peter, 21–22
McFarlane, Robert "Bud," 118, 135, 137, 139–48, 149, 153
McWethy, John, 121
Meese, Edwin III, 60, 87, 99, 106, 130, 153–54
Mental health care, 63
Military spending, 101–2, 172, 173
Mitchell, Aaron, 67
Mondale, Walter, 123–27
Moretti, Bob, 74–75
Morris, Wayne, *33*
Moscow, 170–71
Murphy, George, 59
Music Corporation of America (MCA), 48, 52
Muskie, Edmund, 154
Muslims, 138, 149

Nashua Telegraph, 89
National Press Club, 80
New Hampshire, 82, 88–89

New Right, 87
Nixon, Richard M., 51, 56, 70–72, 78–79, 140
Nofziger, Lynn, 56, 88, 129
North, Oliver, *133*, 135, 143–48, 153, 154, 158
Nuclear deterrence, 162

O'Brien, Pat, 34
O'Connor, Sandra Day, 107–9, *108*
O'Neill, Thomas P., 107

Palestinian Liberation Organization (PLO), 115
Palmer School of Chiropractic, 21, 24
People's Park, 64, *65*
Peres, Shimon, 141
Poindexter, John, 144, 145, 151, 152, 153, 154, 155, 158
Poland, 161
Professional Air Traffic Controllers Organization, 110
Proposition 13, 86

Qaddafi, Muammar al, 114, 146

Rawlings, Marjorie Kinnan, 39
Reagan, Jane (wife), 34, *38*, 39, 43. *See also* Wyman, Jane

Reagan, John Edward "Jack" (father), 9–12, *11*, 19, 20, 26, 31, 36

Reagan, Maureen Elizabeth (daughter), 37, *38*

Reagan, Michael (son), 39

Reagan, Nancy (wife), *47*, 51, *58*, *61*, 68–69, *91*, *120*, 123, 124, 162, 172, *176*. *See also* Davis, Nancy

Reagan, Neil (brother), 10, *11*, 12, 16, 18

Reagan, Nelle Wilson (mother), 10, *11*, 13, 19, 20, 31

Reagan, Patricia Ann (Patti) (daughter), 45, *61*

Reagan, Ronald, *11*, *15*, *23*, *33*, *35*, *42*, *46*, *47*, *55*, *58*, *61*, *65*, *73*, *81*, *91*, *94*, *98*, *104*, *120*, *126*, *136*, *169*, *176*; apology of, 157–59; and arms reduction, 161–71; and assassination attempt, 103–6; cuts in social programs, 173; as favorite-son candidate, 70–72; as governor, 59–78; inauguration of, 91–93; as lifeguard, 13–14; management style of, 60–62, 100; as presidential candidate, 79–84, 90; presidential reelection campaign, 122–27; as radio announcer, 20–27; and Soviet Union, 161–71, 175; staff selection of, 128, 129–31; as student, 12–16; tax cutting of, 66, 101, 175; as "Teflon president," 110–11

Reagan, Ronald Prescott (son), 51, *61*

Reaganomics, 101

Reagan Revolution, 101, 112

Rebates, 75–77

Recession, 175

Regan, Donald T., 100, 130–32, 139, 140, 141, 144–45, 153, 156

Republicans, 51–52

Reykjavik, Iceland, 166–67

Rockefeller, Nelson, 71, 79

Rockne, Knute, 34

Romney, George, 71

Roosevelt, Franklin D., 24, 34, 40

Ruge, Daniel, 106

Sagebrush Rebellion, 109

INDEX

Sandinista Party, 132–34
Saudi Arabia, 135
Savings and loan crisis, 113
Schaller, Michael, 84
Schieffer, Bob, 79
Schultz, George, 99, 116, 135, 141, 144, 145, 151–52, 162, 167, 168
Scowcroft, Brent, 154
Screen Actors Guild, 34, 41–42, 48, 51
Sears, John Patrick, 79, 82, 87, 88–89
Secord, Richard, 135, 145, 146
Sergeant Murphy, 30
Shevardnadze, Eduard, 168
Shiite Muslims, 138
Somoza, Anastasio, 134
Soviet Union, 161–71, 175
Stallion Road, 40
Star Wars. *See* Strategic Defense Initiative
Stockman, Davis, 99, 101, 102, 111–12
Stock market, 170
Strategic Arms Limitation Treaty (SALT II), 162
Strategic Arms Reduction Treaty (START), 170

Strategic Defense Initiative, 163–67
Summit meetings, 129, 160, 164–71
Supply-side economics, 101

Tau Kappa Epsilon fraternity, 16, 18
Tax Reform Act, 131
Taylor, Robert, 27
Terrorists, 132, 138–48, 151
Thatcher, Margaret, 128, *136*
This Is the Army, 39
Tower, John, 154, 157
Tower report, 155–56, 157
TOW missiles, 140–41, 146
"Trickle-down" economics, 101
Tuttle, Holmes, 54

U. S. Embassy, 116
U. S. marines, *117*, 118–19
U. S. Senate, 96, 149
University of California, 63–64
Unruh, Jesse "Big Daddy," 66, 72

Waite, Terry, 151
Wall Street Journal, 125

Walsh, Lawrence, 154, 158, 159, 173
Warner, Jack, 27
Warner Brothers, 28–37
Washington Post, 93, 131
Watt, James, 99–100, 109–10
Wedtech affair, 175
Wee Kirk O'Heather Church, 34
Weinberger, Caspar, 60, 99, 106, 118, 141, 144, 145, 146, 151, 159, 162

Weir, Rev. Benjamin, 143, *150*
Welfare programs, 26, 62, 72–75
WHO, 24
Williams, Larry, 30
Wilson, Bert, 17
WOC, 21–22
Wyman, Jane, 32–34, *33*, *38*. *See also* Reagan, Jane

Yearling, The, 39